CLASSIC SERMONS
ON THE
CROSS OF CHRIST

CLASSIC SERMONS

ON THE

CROSS OF CHRIST

Compiled by
Warren W. Wiersbe

HENDRICKSON
PUBLISHERS

Classic Sermons on the Cross of Christ
Hendrickson Publishers, Inc. edition
ISBN 1-56563-066-1

This edition is published by special arrangement with and permission of Kregel Publications. Copyright © 1990 by Kregel Publications, a division of Kregel, Inc. P.O. Box 2607, Grand Rapids, MI 49501.

Printed in the United States of America

CONTENTS

PREFACE

THE *KREGEL CLASSIC SERMONS SERIES* is an attempt to assemble and publish meaningful sermons from master preachers about significant themes.

These are *sermons*, not essays or chapters taken from books about themes. Not all of these sermons could be called "great," but all of them are *meaningful*. They apply the truths of the Bible to the needs of the human heart, which is something that all effective preaching must do.

While some are better known than others, all of the preachers, whose sermons I have selected, had important ministries and were highly respected in their day. The fact that a sermon is included in this volume does not mean that either the compiler or the publisher agrees with or endorses everything that the man did, preached, or wrote. The sermon is here because it has a valued contribution to make.

These are sermons about *significant* themes. The pulpit is no place to play with trivia. The preacher has thirty minutes in which to help mend broken hearts, change defeated lives, and save lost souls; and he can never accomplish this demanding ministry by distributing homiletical tid-bits. In these difficult days, we do not need "clever" pulpiteers who discuss the times; we need dedicated ambassadors who will preach the eternities.

The reading of these sermons can enrich your own spiritual life. The studying of them can enrich your own skills as an interpreter and expounder of God's truth. However God uses these sermons in your own life and ministry, my prayer is that His Church around the world will be encouraged and strengthened.

WARREN W. WIERSBE

The Death of Christ

Charles Haddon Spurgeon (1834-1892) is undoubtedly the most famous minister of modern times. Converted in 1850, he united with the Baptists and soon began to preach in various places. He became pastor of the Baptist church in Waterbeach in 1851, and 3 years later he was called to the decaying Park Street Church, London. Within a short time, the work began to prosper, a new church was built and dedicated in 1861, and Spurgeon became London's most popular preacher. In 1855, he began to publish his sermons weekly; and today they make up the fifty-seven volumes of *The Metropolitan Tabernacle Pulpit*. He founded a pastor's college and several orphanages.

This sermon is taken from *The New Park Street Pulpit*, volume III, and was preached on January 14, 1858, at the Music Hall, Royal Surrey Gardens.

Charles Haddon Spurgeon

1

THE DEATH OF CHRIST

Yet it pleased the Lord to bruise him; he hath put him to grief: when thou shalt make his soul an offering for sin, he shall see his seed, he shall prolong his days, and the pleasure of the Lord shall prosper in his hand (Isaiah 53:10).

WHAT MYRIADS OF eyes are casting their glances at the sun! What multitudes of men lift up their eyes and behold the starry orbs of heaven! They are continually watched by thousands—but there is one great transaction in the world's history which every day commands far more spectators than that sun which goes forth like a bridegroom, strong to run his race. There is one great event, which every day attracts more admiration than do the sun and moon and stars when they march in their courses. That event is the death of our Lord Jesus Christ. To it the eyes of all the saints who lived before the Christian era were always directed. And backwards, through the thousand years of history, the eyes of all modern saints are looking. Upon Christ, the angels in heaven perpetually gaze. "Which things the angels desire to look into," said Peter (1 Peter 1:12). Upon Christ, the myriad eyes of the redeemed are perpetually fixed; and thousands of pilgrims, through this world of tears, have no higher object for their faith, and no better desire for their vision, than to see Christ as He is in heaven, and in communion to behold His person. Beloved, we shall have many with us, while this morning we turn our face to the Mount of Calvary. We shall not be solitary spectators of the fearful tragedy of our Savior's death. We shall but dart our eyes to that place which is the focus of heaven's joy and delight, the cross of our Lord and Savior Jesus Christ.

Taking our text, then, as a guide, we propose to visit

Calvary, hoping to have the help of the Holy Spirit while we look upon Him who died upon the cross. I would have you notice this morning, first of all, the cause of Christ's death—"It pleased the Lord to bruise him." "It pleased Jehovah to bruise him," says the original; "he hath put him to grief." Second, the reason of Christ's death—"When thou shall make his soul an offering for sin." Christ died because He was an offering for sin. And then, third, the effects and consequences of Christ's death. "He shall see his seed, he shall prolong his days, and the pleasure of the Lord shall prosper in his hand." Come, Sacred Spirit, now, while we attempt to speak on these matchless themes.

The Origin of Christ's Death

"It pleased Jehovah to bruise him; he hath put him to grief." He who reads Christ's life as a mere history traces the death of Christ to the enmity of the Jews and to the fickle character of the Roman governor. In this he acts justly, for the crime and sin of the Savior's death must lay at the door of manhood. This race of ours became a deicide and slew the Lord, nailing its Savior to a tree.

But he who reads the Bible with the eye of faith, desiring to discover its hidden secrets, sees something more in the Savior's death than Roman cruelty or Jewish malice. He sees the solemn decree of God fulfilled by men who were the ignorant but guilty instruments of its accomplishment. He looks beyond the Roman spear and nail, beyond the Jewish taunt and jeer, up to the Sacred Fount, whence all things flow, and he traces the crucifixion of Christ to the breast of Deity. He believes with Peter—"Him, being delivered by the determinate counsel and foreknowledge of God, ye have taken, and by wicked hands have crucified and slain" (Acts 2:23).

We dare not impute to God the sin, but at the same time the fact, with all its marvelous effects in the world's redemption, we must ever trace to the Sacred Fountain of divine love. So does our prophet. He says, "It pleased Jehovah to bruise him." He overlooks both Pilate and Herod, and traces it to the heavenly Father, the first Person in the Divine Trinity. "It pleased the Lord to bruise him; he hath put him to grief."

Now, beloved, there be many who think that God the Father is at best but an indifferent spectator of salvation. Others do belie Him still more. They look upon Him as an unloving, severe Being, who had no love for the human race, and could only be made loving by the death and agonies of our Savior. Now, this is a foul libel upon the fair and glorious grace of God the Father, to whom forever be honor: for Jesus Christ did not die to make God loving, but He died because God was loving.

> 'Twas not to make Jehovah's love
> Towards his people flame,
> That Jesus from the throne above,
> A Suff'ring man became.

> 'Twas not the death which he endured,
> Nor all the pangs he bore,
> That God's eternal love procured,
> For God was love before.

Christ was sent into the world by His Father as the consequence of the Father's affection for His people. Yea, He "so loved the world, that he gave his only betotten Son, that whosoever believeth in him should not perish, but have everlasting life" (John 3:16). The fact is, the Father as much decreed salvation, as much effected it, and as much delighted in it, as did either God the Son or God the Holy Spirit. And when we speak of the Savior of the world, we must always include in that word, if we speak in a large sense, God the Father, God the Son, and God the Holy Spirit, for all these three, as one God, do save us from our sins. The text puts away every hard thought concerning the Father by telling us that it pleased Jehovah to bruise Jesus Christ. The death of Christ is traceable to God the Father. Let us try, if we can, to see that it is so.

It is traceable in decree. God, the one God of heaven and earth, has the book of destiny entirely in His power. In that book there is nothing written by a stranger's hand. The penmanship of the solemn book of predestination is from beginning to end entirely divine.

> Chained to his throne a volume lies,
> With all the fates of men,
> With every angel's form and size
> Drawn by th' eternal pen.

No inferior hand has sketched even so much as the most minute parts of providence. It was all, from its Alpha to its Omega, from its divine preface to its solemn finis, marked out, designed, sketched, and planned by the mind of the all-wise, all-knowing God. Hence, not even Christ's death was exempt from it. He that wings an angel and guides a sparrow, He that protects the hairs of our head from falling prematurely to the ground, was not likely, when He took notice of such little things, to omit in His solemn decrees the greatest wonder of earth's miracles, the death of Christ. No, the blood-stained page of that book, the page that makes both past and future glorious with golden words, that blood-stained page, I say, was as much written of Jehovah as any other.

God determined that Christ should be born of the Virgin Mary, that He should suffer under Pontius Pilate, that He should descend into hades, that thence He should rise again, leading captivity captive, and then should reign forever at the right hand of the Majesty on high. Nay, I know not but that I shall have Scripture for my warrant when I say that this is the very core of predestination, and that the death of Christ is the very center and main-spring by which God did fashion all His other decrees, making this the bottom and foundation-stone upon which the sacred architecture should be built. Christ was put to death by the absolute foreknowledge and solemn decree of God the Father, and in this sense "it pleased the Lord to bruise him; he has put him to grief."

It is traceable to His will. Christ's coming into the world to die was the effect of the Father's will and pleasure. Christ came not into this world unsent. He had laid in Jehovah's bosom from before all worlds, eternally delighting Himself in His Father and being Himself His Father's eternal joy. "In the fulness of time" God did rend His Son from His bosom, His only-begotten Son, and freely delivered Him up for us all. Herein was matchless, peerless love, that the offended judge should permit His co-equal Son to suffer the pains of death for the redemption of a rebellious people.

I want your imaginations for one minute to picture a scene of olden times. There is a bearded patriarch, who rises early in the morning and awakes his son, a young man full of strength, and bids him arise and follow him. They hurry from the house silently and noiselessly, before the mother is awake. They go three days' journey with their men until they come to the Mount of which the Lord has spoken. You know the patriarch. The name of Abraham is always fresh in our memories. On the way, that patriarch speaks not one solitary word to his son. His heart is too full for utterance. He is overwhelmed with grief. God has commanded him to take his son, his only son, and slay him upon the mountain as a sacrifice. They go together; and who shall paint the unutterable anguish of the father's soul, while he walks side by side with the beloved son, of whom he is to be the executioner?

The third day has arrived. The servants are bidden to stay at the foot of the hill while they go to worship God yonder. Now, can any mind imagine how the father's grief must overflow all the banks of his soul, when, as he walked up that hillside, his son said to him, "Father, behold the fire and the wood; but where is the lamb for a burnt offering?" (Genesis 22:7). Can you conceive how he stifled his emotions, and, with sobs, exclaimed, "My son, God will provide himself a lamb?" (v. 8). See! the father has communicated to his son the fact that God has demanded his life. Isaac, who might have struggled and escaped from his father, declares that he is willing to die, if God has decreed it. The father takes his son, binds his hands behind his back, piles up the stones, makes an altar, lays the wood, and has his fire ready.

And now where is the artist who can depict the anguish of the father's countenance when the knife is unsheathed and he holds it up, ready to slay his son? But here the curtain falls. Now the black scene vanishes at the sound of a voice from heaven. The ram caught in the thicket supplies the substitute, and faith's obedience need go no further.

Ah! my brethren. I want to take you from this scene to a far greater one. What faith and obedience made man do, that love constrained God Himself to do. He had but one son, that son His own heart's delight. He covenanted to yield Him up for our redemption, nor did He violate His promise; for, when the fulness of time was come, He sent His Son to be born of the Virgin Mary, that He might suffer for the sins of man. Oh! can you tell the greatness of that love! It made the everlasting God not only put His Son upon the altar, but also actually do the deed and thrust the sacrificial knife into His Son's heart! Can you think how overwhelming must have been the love of God toward the human race when He completed in act what Abraham only did in intention? Look ye there, and see the place where His only Son hung dead upon the cross, the bleeding victim of awakened justice! Here is love indeed! Here we see how it was that it pleased the Father to bruise him.

It is traceable to God's hand. This allows me to push my text just one point further. Beloved, it is not only true that God did design and did permit with willingness the death of Christ; it is, moreover, true that the unutterable agonies that clothed the death of the Savior with superhuman terror were the effect of the Father's bruising of Christ in very act and deed.

There is a martyr in prison. The chains are on his wrists, and yet he sings. It has been announced to him that tomorrow is his burning day. He claps his hands right merrily, and he smiles while he says, "It will be sharp work tomorrow, I shall breakfast below on fiery tribulations, but afterwards I will sup with Christ. Tomorrow is my wedding-day, the day for which I have long panted, when I shall sign the testimony of my life by a glorious death." The time is come; the men with the halberds precede him through the streets. Mark the serenity of the martyr's countenance. He turns to some who look upon him, and exclaims, "I value these iron chains far more than if they had been of gold; it is a sweet thing to die for Christ." Around the stake are gathered a few of the boldest of the saints, and as he unrobes himself—before he stands upon the faggots to receive his doom—he tells them that it is a joyous thing to be a soldier of Christ, to be allowed to give his body to be burned. He shakes hands with them and bids them "Good bye" with merry cheer. One would think he were going to a bridal, rather than to be burned. He steps upon the faggots; the chain is put about his middle. After a brief word of prayer, as soon as the fire begins to ascend, he speaks to the people with manful boldness. But hark! He sings while the faggots are cracking and the smoke is blowing upward. He sings, and when his nether parts are burned, he still goes on chanting sweetly some psalm of old. "God is our refuge and strength, a very present help in trouble; therefore will we not fear, though the earth be removed and though the mountains be carried into the midst of the sea" (Psalm 46:1, 2). *In our Times of sufferings*

Picture another scene. There is the Savior going to His cross, all weak and wan with suffering; His soul is sick and sad within Him. There is no divine composure there. So sad is His heart that He faints in the streets. The Son of God faints beneath a cross that many a criminal might have carried. They nail Him to the tree. There is no song of praise. He is lifted up in the air, and there He hangs preparatory to His death. You hear no shout of exultation. There is a stern compression of His face, as if unutterable agony were tearing His heart—as if over again Gethsemane were being

acted on the cross—as if His soul were still saying, "If
it be possible let this cross pass from me; nevertheless,
not as I will, but as thou wilt" (Matthew 26:39).

Hark! He speaks. Will He not sing sweeter songs
than ever came from martyr's lips? Ah! no; it is an
awful wail of woe that can never be imitated. "My God,
my God, why hast thou forsaken me?" (Matthew 27:46).
The martyrs said not that: God was with them.
Confessors of old cried not so, when they came to die.
They shouted in their fires, and they praised God on
their racks. Why this? Why does the Savior suffer so?
Why, beloved, it was because the Father bruised Him.
That sunshine of God's countenance that has cheered
many a dying saint was withdrawn from Christ. The
consciousness of acceptance with God, which has made
many a holy man espouse the cross with joy, was not
afforded to our Redeemer. Therefore He suffered in
thick darkness of mental agony. Read Psalm 22, and
learn how Jesus suffered. Pause over the solemn words
in verses 1, 2, 6, and following.

Underneath the Church are the everlasting arms;
but underneath Christ there were no arms at all.
Instead, His Father's hand pressed heavily against Him;
the upper and the nether millstones of divine wrath
pressed and bruised Him; and not one drop of joy or
consolation was afforded to Him. "It pleased Jehovah
to bruise him; he hath put him to grief." This, my
brethren, was the climax of the Savior's woe, that His
Father turned away from Him, and put Him to grief.

I expounded the first part of the subject—the origin
of our Savior's worst suffering, the Father's pleasure.

The Reason for Christ's Death

Our second point must explain the first, otherwise it
is an insolvable mystery how God should bruise His
Son, who was perfect innocence, while poor fallible
confessors and martyrs have had no such bruising from
Him in the time of their trial. What was the reason fo
the Savior's suffering? We are told here, "Thou shalt

Christ — The Evening Sacrifice.
The offering for Sin in form of Substitute

make his soul an offering for sin." Christ was thus troubled because His soul was an offering for sin.

Now, I am going to be as plain as I can, while I preach over again the precious doctrine of the atonement of Christ Jesus our Lord. Christ was an offering for sin in the sense of a substitute. God longed to save; but, if such a word may be allowed, justice tied His hands. "I must be just," said God. "That is a necessity of my nature. Stern as fate, and fast as immutability, is the truth that I must be just. But then My heart desires to forgive—to pass by man's transgressions and pardon them."

How can it be done? Wisdom stepped in, and said, "It shall be done thus," and Love agreed with Wisdom. "Christ Jesus, the Son of God, shall stand in man's place, and He shall be offered upon Mount Calvary instead of man. Now, when you see Christ going up the Mount of Doom, you see man going there; when you see Christ hurled upon His back, upon the wooden cross, you see the whole company of His elect there; and when you see the nails driven through His blessed hands and feet, it is the whole body of His Church who there, in their substitute, are nailed to the tree. Now the soldiers lift the cross and dash it down into the socket prepared for it. Every one of His bones is dislocated, and His body is thus torn with agonies that cannot be described. 'Tis manhood suffering there; 'tis the Church suffering there, in the substitute. And when Christ dies, you are to look upon the death of Christ, not as His own dying merely, but as the dying of all those for whom He stood as the scapegoat and the substitute.

It is true, Christ died really Himself; it is equally true that He did not die for Himself, but died as the substitute, in the room, place, and stead of all believers. When you die, you will die for yourselves; when Christ died, He died for you, if you be a believer in Him. When you pass through the gates of the grave, you go there solitary and alone; you are not the representative of a body of men, but you pass through the gates of

The Ultimate Sacrifice — the soldiers died for himself cannot save others your god will be remembered Christ (Substitute died)
Go or ask but Salvation is thru Christ

death as an individual. But remember, when Christ went through the sufferings of death, He was the representative Head of all His people.

Understand, then, the sense in which Christ was made a sacrifice for sin. But here lies the glory of this matter. It was as a substitute for sin that He did actually and literally suffer punishment for the sin of all His elect. When I say this, I am not to be understood as using any figure whatever, but as saying actually what I mean. For his sin, man was condemned to eternal fire. When God took Christ to be the substitute, it is true that He did not send Christ into eternal fire. But He poured upon Him grief so desperate that it was a valid payment for even an eternity of fire. Man was condemned to live forever in hell. God did not send Christ forever into hell, but He placed on Christ a punishment that was equivalent for that. Although He did not give Christ to drink the actual hells of believers, yet He gave Him a *quid pro quo*—something that was equivalent thereunto. He took the cup of Christ's agony, and He put in there suffering, misery, and anguish, such as only God can imagine or dream of. It was the exact equivalent for all the suffering, all the woe, and all the eternal tortures of everyone who shall at last stand in heaven, bought with the blood of Christ.

Perhaps you say, "Did Christ drink it all to its dregs?" Did He suffer it all? Yes, my brethren, He took the cup, and,

> At one triumphant draught of love,
> He drank damnation dry.

He suffered all the horror of hell. In one pelting shower of iron wrath it fell upon Him with hailstones bigger than a talent; and He stood until the black cloud had emptied itself completely. There was our debt, huge and immense; He paid the utmost farthing of whatever His people owed. And now there is not so much as a doit or a farthing due to the justice of God in the way of punishment from any believer. Although we owe God gratitude, although we owe much to His love, we owe nothing to His justice; for Christ in that hour took all our sins, past, present, and future. He was punished for them all there and then, that we might never be punished, because He suffered in our stead. Do you see, then, how it was that God the Father bruised Him? Unless He had so done, the agonies of Christ could not have been an equivalent for our sufferings; for hell consists in the hiding of God's face from sinners, and if God had not hidden His face from Christ, Christ could not—I see not how He could—have endured any suffering that could have been accepted as an equivalent for the woes and agonies of His people.

I can hear some doubting one ask, "Do you mean us to understand this atonement that you have now preached as being a literal fact?" I say, most solemnly, I do. There are in the world many theories of atonement. But I cannot see any atonement in any one, except in this doctrine of substitution.

Many divines say that Christ did something when He died that enabled God to be just and yet be the Justifier of the ungodly. What that something is they do not tell us. They believe in an atonement made for everybody; but then, their atonement is just this. They believe that Judas was atoned for just as much as Peter; they believe that the damned in hell were as much an object of Jesus Christ's satisfaction as the saved in heaven. Also, although they do not say it in proper words, yet they must mean it, for it is a fair inference that in the case of multitudes, Christ died in vain, for He died for them all, they say. Yet so ineffectual was His dying for them, that though He died for them they are damned afterwards. Now, such an atonement I despise—I reject it.

I may be called Antinomian or Calvinist for preaching a limited atonement; but I had rather believe a limited atonement that is efficacious for all men for whom it was intended, than an universal atonement that is not efficacious for anybody, except the will of man be joined with it. Why, my brethren, if we were only so far atoned for by the death of Christ that any one of us might afterwards save himself, Christ's atonement were not worth a farthing, for there is not man of us can save himself—no not under the gospel. If I am to be saved by faith, if that faith is to be my own act, unassisted by the Holy Spirit, I am as unable to save myself by faith as to save myself by good works. And after all, though men call this a limited atonement, it is as effectual as their own fallacious and rotten redemptions can pretend to be.

But do you know the limit of it? Christ has bought a "multitude, which no man can number" (Revelation 7:9). The limit of it is just this: He has died for sinners; whoever in this congregation inwardly and sorrowfully knows himself to be a sinner, Christ died for him. Whoever seeks Christ shall know that Christ died for him; for our sense of need of Christ and our seeking after Christ are infallible proofs that Christ died for us. And, mark, here is something substantial. The Arminian says Christ died for him; and then, poor man, he has but small consolation therefrom, for he says, "Ah! Christ died for me; that does not prove much. It only proves I may be saved if I mind what I am after. I may perhaps forget myself; I may run into sin, and I may perish. Christ has done a good deal for me, but not quite enough, unless I do something." But the man who receives the Bible as it is, he says, "Christ died for me, then my eternal life is sure. I know," says he, "that Christ cannot be punished in a man's stead, and the man be punished afterwards. No," says he, "I believe in a just God, and if God be just, he will not punish Christ first, and then punish men afterwards. No, my Savior died, and now I am free from every demand of God's vengeance, and I can walk through this world secure. No thunderbolt can smite me, and I can die absolutely certain that for me there is no flame of hell, and no pit digged; for Christ my ransom suffered in my stead, and, therefore, am I clean delivered.

Oh! glorious doctrine! I would wish to die preaching it! What better testimony can we bear to the love and faithfulness of God than the testimony of a substitution eminently satisfactory for all them that believe on Christ? I will here quote the testimony of that preeminently profound divine, Dr. John Owen:

"Redemption is the freeing of a man from misery by the intervention of a ransom. Now, when a ransom is paid for the liberty of a prisoner, does not justice demand that he should have and enjoy the liberty so purchased for him by a valuable consideration? If I should pay a thousand pounds for a man's deliverance from bondage to him that detains him, who has power to set us free and is contented with the price I give, were it not injurious to me and the poor prisoner that his deliverance be not accomplished? Can it possibly be conceived that there should be a redemption of men, and those men not redeemed? Or that a price should be paid, and the purchase not consummated? Yet all this must be made true, and innumerable other absurdities, if universal redemption be asserted. A price is paid for all, yet few delivered; the redemption of all consummated, yet few of them redeemed; the judge satisfied, the jailer conquered, and yet the prisoners enthralled!

"Doubtless, *universal*, and *redemption*, where the greatest part of men perish, are as irreconcilable as *Roman* and *Catholic*. If there be a universal redemption of all, then all men are redeemed. If they are redeemed, then are they delivered from all misery, virtually or actually, whereunto they were enthralled, and that by the intervention of a ransom. Why, then, are not all saved? In a word, the redemption wrought by Christ being the full deliverance of the persons redeemed from all misery, wherein they were enwrapped, by the price of His blood, it cannot possibly be conceived to be universal unless all be saved: so that the opinion of the Universalists is unsuitable to redemption."

I pause once more; for I hear some timid soul say, "But, sir, I am afraid I am not elect, and if so, Christ did not die for me." Stop, sir! Are you a sinner? Do you feel it? Has God the Holy Spirit made you feel that you are a lost sinner? Do you want salvation? If you do not want it, it is no hardship that it is not provided for you; but if you really feel that you want it, you are God's elect. If you have a desire to be saved, a desire given you of the Holy Spirit, that desire is a token for good. If you have begun believingly to pray for salvation, you have therein a sure evidence that you are saved. Christ was punished for you. And if now you can say, "Nothing in my hands I bring, simply to the cross I cling," you may be as sure you are God's elect as you are sure of your own existence; for this is the infallible proof of election—a sense of need and a thirst after Christ.

The Blessed Effects of Christ's Death

And now I have just to conclude by noticing the blessed effects of the Savior's death. On this I shall be very brief.

The first effect of the Savior's death is, "He shall see his seed." Men shall be saved by Christ. Men have offspring by life; Christ had an offspring by death. Men die and leave their children, and they see not their seed; Christ lives, and every day sees His seed brought into the unity of the faith. One effect of Christ's death is the salvation of multitudes. Notice, this is, not a chance salvation. When Christ died, the angel did not say, as some have represented him, "Now by his death many may be saved." The word of prophecy had quenched all "buts" and "peradventures." "By his righteousness he shall justify many" (see Isaiah 53). There was not so much as an atom of chance-work in the Savior's death. Christ knew what He bought when He died; and what He bought He will have—that, and no more, and no less. There is no effect of Christ's death that is left to peradventure. "Shalls" and "wills" made the covenant fast: Christ's bloody death shall effect its solemn purpose. Every heir of grace shall meet around the throne, "Shall bless the wonders of his grace, And make his glories known."

The second effect of Christ's death is, "He shall prolong his day." Yes, bless His name, when He died He did not end His life. He could not long be held a prisoner in the tomb. The third morning came, and the conqueror, rising from His sleep, burst the iron bonds of death and came forth from His prison-house, no more to die. He waited His 40 days, and then with shouts of sacred song, He "led captivity captive and ascended up on high" (Ephesians 4:8). "In that he died he died unto sin once; but in that he liveth, he liveth unto God" (Romans 6:10), no more to die.

> Now by his Father's side he sits,
> And there triumphant reigns,
> the conqueror over death and hell.

And, last of all, by Christ's death the Father's good pleasure was effected and prospered. God's good pleasure is that this world shall one day be totally redeemed from sin; God's good pleasure is that this poor planet, so long swathed in darkness, shall soon shine out in brightness, like a new-born sun. Christ's death has done it. The stream that flowed from His side on Calvary shall cleanse the world from all its blackness. That house of midday darkness was the rising of a new sun of righteousness, which shall never cease to shine upon the earth.

Yes, the hour is coming when swords and spears shall be forgotten things—when the harness of war and the pageantry of pomp shall all be laid aside for the food of the worm or the contemplation of the curious. The hour approaches when old Rome shall shake upon her seven hills, when Mohammed's crescent shall wane to wax no more, when all the gods of the heathens shall lose their thrones and be cast out to the moles and to the bats. Then, from the equator to the poles Christ shall be honored, the Lord paramount of earth. From land to land, from the river even to the ends of the earth, one King shall reign, one shout shall be raised, "Hallelujah, hallelujah, the Lord God Omnipotent reigneth." Then, my brethren, shall it be seen what Christ's death has accomplished; for "the pleasure of the Lord shall prosper in his hand."

He Dies. He Must Die.

William E. Sangster (1900-1960) was the "John Wesley" of his generation, for he devoted his life to evangelism and the promoting of practical sanctification. He pastored in England and Wales, and his preaching ability attracted the attention of the Methodist leaders. He ministered during World War II at Westminster Central Hall, London, where he pastored the church, managed an air-raid shelter in the basement, and studied for his Ph.D. at the London University! He served as president of the Methodist Conference (1950) and director of the denomination's home missions and evangelism ministry. He published several books on preaching, sanctification, and evangelism, as well as volumes of sermons.

This message comes from *Sangster's Special-day Sermons*, published in 1960 by Abingdon Press and used by permission of his son.

William E. Sangster

2

HE DIES. HE MUST DIE.

Behoved it not the Christ to suffer these things? (Luke 24:26).

WE OFTEN SPEAK of the cross as stark and unrelieved tragedy—as the most awful, wicked, and incongruous thing that ever happened on this planet. And, in a sense, we are right. Almighty God comes to earth, lives as a man among men . . . and He is whipped, spat upon, pierced with nails, and hung up naked for leprous sinners and painted harlots to jeer at. It is too shocking to be credible.

> He laid His glory by,
> He wrapped Him in our clay;
> Unmarked by human eye,
> The latent Godhead lay.
> And when He did that, we
> . . . set at nought and sold Him,
> Pierced and nailed Him to the tree.

I marvel that even in hell they could think of anything so fiendishly wicked as that. It was, indeed, the most incongruous thing that ever happened on the planet.

A Vast Incongruity, A Lovely Congruity

And yet, while that is true, it is only half the truth. In all the awful incongruity, I perceive a congruity as well. In the midst of its shocking unfitness, I see a fitness too. A fitness in the cross! I learned it from my Lord Himself in the first explanation He ever made about His dying after He had risen from the dead. Walking to Emmaus with two disciples who did not recognize Him and who were stunned by all that happened on Calvary, He was at pains to explain to them why the cross had to be. He said, "Behoved it not the Christ to suffer these things?" (Luke 24:26). Can't you see the fittingness of it? Don't you see that it is the keystone of the arch?

And when I got that word from Jesus, I raced through the rest of the New Testament to find confirmation in other parts of Scripture for the interpretation I gave to that word. The confirmation was there. I started with the epistle to the Hebrews and I read of Jesus: "It behoved Him in all things to be made like unto His brethren" (Hebrews 2:17). He had to suffer. It behoved Him. I should have guessed it.

I read of the Father in the same epistle: "It became Him to make the author of their salvation perfect through suffering" (Hebrews 2:10). It became Him. It was fitting.

So there it is. The sublime paradox again. A great crime; a great love. A vast incongruity; a lovely congruity. The world's worst; heaven's best.

> O love of God! O sin of man!
> In this dread act your strength is tried;
> And victory remains with love:
> For He, our Lord, is crucified.

And then, I look still farther afield to find confirmation of this truth. John Wesley, as you may recall, had two simple tests for any teaching he gave to people, and he expected the tests to corroborate each other. "Is it in the Bible?" he asked first. And then: "Is it in experience?"

I find this strange teaching of the fittingness of the cross in the Bible. Can I find that teaching in life as well?

I find it in life as well! Sacrifice is written all over life. It runs like a scarlet thread through all our racial history and all our personal history too. The cross isn't a queer incongruity that occurred in history only on the first Good Friday. To those who have insight, it has been in this strange life of ours from the beginning. What did the author of the book of Revelation mean

when he said, "A Lamb slain from the foundation of
the world"? (13:8). The cross is in life—all life. It has
been in life from the beginning—from the foundation
of the world. It is, indeed, so much in life that you
could call it the foundation itself, the ground-plan of
the universe. Our life is all reared on a cross.

I once took a small boy into a cathedral. We entered
by the west door, and as our eyes grew accustomed to
the dim light, he looked up above the rood-screen and
he said, "There is a cross up there." I pointed to the
floor of the cathedral and said, "There is a cross down
here." The cathedral was a cross. Of course! It was a
cruciform building. Chancel and nave for the upright;
transept and transept for the cross-beam. It was all
cross.

You can take me to Golgotha and say, "There is a
cross up there." I point you to earth and say, "There is
a cross down here." The cross is inherent in life. It is
life's foundation. It is not an incongruity. Your Savior
is focusing in a moment of time a fact that is timeless,
and on the first Good Friday the Lamb slain from the
foundation of the world is seen slain. What a mystery!
How shall we pierce into the heart of this?

The cross is in all life. It is in the earth; the seed
dies that the plant may live. It is in the landscape; the
mountain is bare and barren that the vale may be rich
and fecund. The valleys stand so thick with corn. Aye,
they do! And they do it by the soil washed from the
mountain. The cross is in your blood. What are the
white corpuscles doing in your blood-stream? Watching
for infection! When they find it, they absorb it, but
they too, in their turn, must be absorbed by the newly
created cells which take their place, or the blood would
stagnate and the body would die.

I say again: the cross is not one vast incongruity. It
is the red element in all life, but in Jesus on the cross
it is placarded before your eyes. It has a terrible fitness
in this world. Listen to Him explaining it Himself to
those two men on the way to Emmaus: "Behoved it not
the Christ to suffer these things?" Wasn't it fitting?
Could it have been avoided?

It couldn't have been avoided. Not by the Savior.
He did not come to judge the word,
He did not come to blame;
He did not only come to seek,
It was to save He came;
And when we call Him Savior,
Then we call Him by His Name.

Let us see if we can understand a little more clearly why the cross was necessary. We shall not understand it all. The deep mystery will elude our probing, but some gleam of understanding will come as we gaze.

I will put it to you as questions.

Question 1

Could any but a crucified Savior reveal our sins? It is a recurrent tragedy of our race that we do not realize the sinfulness of sin. We call our sins "mistakes," "weaknesses," "slips," and even when we use the right word—*sin*—we use it lightly. What is sin?

This is sin! It is sins that takes the holy God—incarnate here on earth—and treats Him as no beast should be treated. It is sin that takes the gracious loving Jesus, who never harmed a soul and spent all His days in helping and healing, and strips Him, lashes Him, spits on Him, pierces Him with nail . . . and then laughs at Him. That is sin. Your sin. O yes! your sin. You have been guilty of the same sins that nailed Him to the cross. Gossip, greed, bigotry, fear, slander . . . they added up to this. You have gossiped, been greedy, bigoted, fearful, and slanderous. You didn't think it would come to this in the end. It took the cross to make you realize what sin really was.

Sin is deadly. It is the one thing God won't tolerate. The war between good and evil is to the death. And you lend yourself to sin without knowing to what dirty enterprise you have sold yourself . . . until you see that cross.

Whenever you are tempted to feel that it is only a "white lie;" whenever you catch yourself saying: "Well, one must look after oneself;" whenever you are greedy, slanderous, loose in speech, selfish and grasping . . . look at the cross. That shows its real nature. Sin isn't an invention of preachers. Sin does that . . . and you would never have known its deadly nature had He not endured to be placarded before your eyes.

Have you ever seen the germs that cause disease magnified for examination? They are most interesting to look at. They have such curious shapes; even beautiful shapes, some of them. It is possible to take an artist's interest in them and half forget the deadly nature they possess.

But now go straight from that magnified specimen-glass and see the germ at its deadly work in the hospital ward. Look! This is Lupus at work. You were specially drawn to that magnified bacillus. It seemed so innocent; even pleasing to look upon.

Yet that germ is doing this; it is eating that man's living flesh away. On and on it goes and nothing, it seems, can arrest it. You didn't know the deadly character of that bacillus when you first looked at it. It seemed just "cute," and you could discuss it with academic detachment. But what does it do? It does this!

So it is with sin. You can discuss it academically. You can even argue whether there is such a thing or not, or whether it is all the imagination of moralists.

But then go and look at the cross. It does that. It is the most deadly thing known to God and man. It would slay the body and damn the soul. It is hell's worst. You can see it when you gaze upon the cross.

Question 2

Could any but a crucified Savior save us from our sins? It seems not. The New Testament is quite emphatic on this point. Without shedding of blood there is no remission. It is death that gives life.

Now, why that should be I do not know, and I don't think anybody else does but God Himself. The New Testament has no theories about the atonement. It has the atonement—but not an explanation.

That is often the case in the Bible. The Bible begins right away by talking about God. "In the beginning, God . . ." (Genesis 1:1), but it never sets out to prove Him. The Bible everywhere assumes man's moral freedom, but nowhere does it seek to explain it. The Bible always speaks with authority of God's Book, but never self-consciously. It never sets out to prove by argument that it is a Book apart.

And so with the atonement. It is there. Plain. Repeated. Emphatic. "Without shedding of blood there is no remission" (Hebrews 9:22). But it never says "why."

I wonder if that hint I gave just now will give us the clue that we are seeking? The cross is inherent in all life. No life without death. There is sacrifice woven into the very fabric of our days. It is in the earth; it is in the landscape; it is in our blood...all life illustrates and reaches out for that divine principle in the universe. It is here eternally in God. You may see it in a moment of time. The Lamb slain from the foundation of the world is seen slain, and by His stripes we are healed.

Find time during this solemn day to sit quietly before the cross. Just sit and look and meditate on the passion hymns.

> Five bleeding wounds He bears,
> Received on Calvary;
> They pour effectual prayers,
> They strongly speak for me:
> Forgive him, O forgive! they cry,
> Nor let that ransomed sinner die!
> You see? It is the bleeding wounds which cry.
> Forgive him, O forgive! they cry,
> Nor let that ransomed sinner die!
> O let me kiss Thy bleeding feet,
> And bathe and wash them with my tears!
> The story of Thy love repeat
> In every drooping sinner's ears,
> That all may hear the quickening sound,
> Since I, even I, have mercy found.

And, as you sit and gaze, it will be borne in upon you that only a crucified Savior could meet your need.

Canon Peter Green tells of how he came out of his church in Salford one day and saw a young working man staring incredulously at a crucifix. When he saw the parson, the young man said, "I don't see what good it done the Father that His Son should die like that." What a confusion of ideas lies behind that remark. It wasn't the good of the Father; it was the good of undone sinners that led our Lord to die upon the wood. And, in His well-beloved Son, the Father suffered too. If you say that God required the penalty, you must at least say that God paid it. Make no division in the Godhead. It is bound to be false.

> For you and for me
> He prayed on the tree:
> The prayer is accepted, the sinner is free.
> That sinner am I,
> Who on Jesus Rely,
> And come for the pardon God cannot deny.

Question 3

Could any but a crucified Savior meet us in our agony? I have learned nothing in more than 30 years of ministry if I have not learned that there are tears in things. When life is at the spring and love is young and one is fit, how sweet and engaging life seems. Anybody who takes a somber view of life is thought to be a dull pessimist unable to see this lovely life as it is.

Those who see this life as it is see the tears in things. Enjoy it while you can. Seize every scrap of legitimate happiness, but remember . . . life is not a picnic. There are tears in things.

Every day the undertaker plies his solemn trade. Every day hearts break. Every day the routine goes on in a thousand hospitals; the cancer hospitals; the homes for blind babies; the homes for the epileptics...and on and on it goes. You who are healthy and happy; you can forget those things. I am glad, in a way, you can. But those of us who see life whole, we cannot.

I was in Macclesfield a while ago, and as we ran through the town I was impressed by a great institution:

one part of it so modern, with colorful green tiles, and one part of it old; but all of it so extensive. It seemed to take the car quite a while to pass by. "What a place!" I said to my friends. "What a huge place!"

"Yes," they said. "It is the mental hospital."

The mental hospital! That saddest of all sicknesses. There are tears in things.

Every week the minister must meet the broken-hearted. I say again: you may forget it; we can't.

If I had no crucified Savior with which to greet those who have been broken by the tragedies of life, I would not know what to say to them. How could I speak to that girl whose young husband was killed on their honeymoon? How could I speak to those parents whose longed-for child turned out to be a cretin? How could I speak to that poor polio victim 20 years in an iron lung? How could one speak to the multitude of sufferers in a world like this if one had no crucified Savior to speak about?

To all those whose minds reel in sorrow; to all those who feel resentful because life has done to them its worst; to all those tempted to believe there is no God in heaven, or, at least, no God of love, He comes and He shows them His hands. More eloquently than any words, those pierced hands say, "I have suffered."

There are tears in things . . . and there were tears on the face of Jesus Christ. Not for His own suffering, but for that of others, is it not recorded that Jesus wept?

He weeps with the sufferers still; with you who are suffering, and whose hearts may be bitter and resentful, even while I speak to you.

You can't steel yourself against this suffering life. You need the "inside word" He brings. Can you resist the appeal of those eyes "majestic after death"?

He has suffered. He knows the answers. He could bring even you to utter peace.

"Behoved it not the Christ to suffer these things?" Wasn't it fitting? Can't you see it had to be?

NOTES

The Power of the Cross

John Henry Jowett (1864-1923) was known as "the greatest preacher in the English-speaking world." Born in Yorkshire, England, he was ordained into the Congregational ministry. His second pastorate was at the famous Carr's Lane Church, Birmingham, where he followed the eminent Dr. Robert W. Dale. From 1911-18, he pastored the Fifth Avenue Presbyterian Church, New York City; and from 1918-23, he ministered at Westminster Chapel, London, succeeding G. Campbell Morgan.

He wrote many books of devotional messages and sermons. This message comes from *Apostolic Optimism*, published in 1930 by Richard R. Smith, Inc.

John Henry Jowett

3

THE POWER OF THE CROSS

For the Jews require a sign, and the Greeks seek after wisdom: But we preach Christ crucified, unto the Jews a stumblingblock, and unto the Greeks foolishness; but unto them which are called, both Jews and Greeks, Christ the power of God, and the wisdom of God (1 Corinthians 1:22-24).

"THE JEWS ASK for signs." That's a request which is not necessarily indicative of a thirst; it may be an asking behind which there is no parched and aching spirit. That is the bane and peril of all externalism. It may gratify a feverish curiosity without awakening the energies of a holy life. The Jews asked for signs. "Now, when Herod saw Jesus he was exceedingly glad" (Luke 23:8), for he hoped to see a sign. It was a restless curiosity, itching for the sensation of some novel entertainment; it was not the pang of a faint and weary heart hungering for bread. "He answered him nothing" (Luke 23:9). "The Jews ask for signs," a request which is frequently indicative of a life of moral alienation. Externalism bounds in moral opiates, and externalisms men often discover drugs by which they benumb the painful sense of their own excesses. "A wicked and an adulterous generation seeketh after a sign" (Matthew 12:39). Men try to resolve into merely physical sensations and sensationalisms what can only be apprehended by the delicate tender tendrils of a penitent and aspiring soul.

"And the Greeks seek after wisdom." They are the epicures in philosophies, the dainty tasters of intellectual subtleties. They are the experts who relish speculative cleverness, whose mouths water at the airiest abstractions, and who recoil from the severely practical in stern disgust and contempt. "The Jews ask for signs," and their religion degenerates into a despiritualized system of magic. "The Greeks seek after wisdom," and their religion becomes the domain of the disciplinist theorist, the heritage of a cultured and exclusive aristocracy. "But we preach Christ crucified," proclaiming what appears to be His shame, glorying in what appears to be the hour of His collapse, emphasizing the season of His appalling darkness, obtruding the bloody, unadorned, and undecked cross on which He suffered His apparent defeat. "We preach Christ crucified"—we do not whisper it. "We preach Christ crucified"—we do not whisper it in secret coteries; we do not timidly submit it for subdued discussion in the academic grove; we do not offer it to the hands of exclusive circles—we preach it, we stand out like the town crier in the public way, and we proclaim it to the common and indiscriminate crowd. "The Jews ask for signs; we preach Christ crucified, unto the Jews a stumblingblock." They cannot get over it; it obtrudes itself like a barrier right athwart the common track of their common thought; it throws all their reckonings into confusion; it confronts their hunger for a novel entertainment by an apparent stone. Christ crucified! A sign! It is significant of nothing but shame, failure, utter and dishonorable defeat.

"The Greeks seek after wisdom; we preach Christ crucified, unto the Greeks foolishness." It offended their mental pride, it confronted their speculative ingenuity as a piece of unmitigated absurdity, and they repelled it, repelled it because it did not approach and conciliate their interest in the graceful robes of an alluring philosophy. To the Jews a stumbling block, to the Greeks an absurdity; but "to them that are called," to them who offer it the hospitality of mind and heart, to them who reverently entertain it on the plea of its own august claims, to them who render it the willing homage and obedience of the will, "to them that are called, both Jews and Greeks," irrespective of nationality or race, "Christ, the power of God," a mighty dynamic which is the pledge of all moral spiritual triumph, "and the wisdom of God," an illumination in which the reverent soul is led into the secret hallowed precincts of the very Light of Life.

"We preach Christ crucified," says Paul, and we are not going to be diverted by the hunger for mere sensation. "We preach Christ crucified," and we are not going to be disengaged from our high calling and tempted to submit our Gospel as a piece of subtle and mincing controversy. We preach it boldly, definitely—"Christ, and Him crucified." It was the only Gospel for our own.

Why Preach Christ Crucified?

Christ crucified preserves the sense of God's holiness. I want to lead your thoughts round about this great text, and to ask you to consider with me why it is that the gospel of Christ and Him crucified is the only redeeming message for our own day. We preach Christ crucified because it is the doctrine that incomparably preserves for us the sense of the holiness of God. Now, is that altogether an irrelevant and particularly inopportune word to apply to our own day? I think that the sense of the holiness of God is an element that is conspicuously lacking in our modern religious life. One misses it in our prayers. It is by no means pronounced in our latest hymns. Its presence is not indicated by any pronounced signs in our life. Our ears do not seem to be as open to the cry of the seraphim, "Holy, holy, holy is the Lord of Hosts."

I turn to the Old Testament, and I find men lying prostrate in the dust, while they cry in most fruitful wonder, "Holy, holy, holy." I turn to the Revelation, to those mystic glimpses of life in the unseen; and wherever I turn my eyes are smitten with the oft-repeated cry, "Holy, holy, holy." "They have no rest," says John, "They have no rest day nor night, saying, Holy, holy, holy" (Revelation 4:8).

I take up great works of devotion, great manuals and helpmeets of devotion, and I find that every devotional exercise is prefaced by an attempt to realize the awful holiness of God. Take down from your shelves Lancelot Andrewes' great *Book of Private Devotion*, a book to which I personally and privately owe much more than I can ever tell you. How does each day's exercise begin? In what he calls meditation and adoration. Why, the very words have an old-world flavor about them as though they belonged to a long past and obsolete day. Meditation, adoration! Lancelot Andrewes leads us in this meditation and adoration right up to the great White Throne, into the awful stillness of the holy place, and instinctively you feel you must take the shoes off your feet, that you must silence every loud trampling frivolity and flippancy, that the very stillness may steep its message into your awakened and wondering spirit. Then Lancelot Andrewes leads from adoration and meditation to confession, and I do not wonder that such meditations are followed by such confessions, and such contemplations by such agonizing cries, such visions by such tears.

But, brethren, that is a very silent note in our day. This never-silent emphasis in Scripture, and this essential preface to all great books of devotion, are not to be found in very pronounced emphasis in our modern religious life. I do not think that the cry rings through our ears today as it did through the ears of the saints of old—"Holy, holy, holy, Lord God Almighty." The God whom we commonly conceive is lax, loose, kindly, easy-going, and good-natured; a God with whom we dare to trifle, a God with whom we dare to take liberties without being afraid of the consuming flame—an easy-going God. Why should I fear? God is love. Why should I take the shoes from my feet? And so, my brethren, there are a number of words that have become almost obsolete; they are quite dropping out of our religious vocabulary—awe, fear, trembling, and reverence.

We may not like the words, we may be very happy that they have become obsolete, but the great realities which the words portray will have to be restored to our religious thought. The conception of the holiness of God must not be relegated to primitive times as though it belonged to the merely immature thinkings of the old dispensation: it is an equally cardinal revelation of the new. The idea of Fatherhood does not exclude or obscure the idea of holiness; it includes and intensifies it. Our Master Himself, in a word which I think is far more pregnant than we are inclined to suppose—our Master Himself took the two words, and sought, for our infinite advantage, to reveal their eternal wedlock when He cried "Holy Father" (John 17:11). It is the first of the two words I want to have re-enthroned—"Holy Father."

If I want to gaze upon the holiness of God, I knew no place like the cross. Nowhere else do I see—speaking now not as a preacher, speaking now as a disciple— nowhere else do I see, as I see at the cross, the wondrous purity of the great White Throne. Nowhere do I more find such fruitful stillness as when I am near the cross. Nowhere do I feel so inclined to take the shoes from off my feet. And how do you account for it?

I stood in a Roman Catholic chapel a day or two ago, in the Oratory in Birmingham, where Cardinal Newman finished his days. I stood just under the figure of the crucified Christ. I do not know that it helped me better to realize my Master's love for me, but I noticed that the steps which formed the pediment were worn with the knees of praying folk. I wonder how it is we are so still when we get near the cross! May it not be because we are instinctively sensitive that we are very near the great White Throne, and that there, in the supreme revelation of the eternal holiness?

My brethren, I plead that we may get that note back into our religious life. We are never going to have grand trees of righteousness until they are rooted in a rich soil of reverence, and we are never, I think, going to get the requisite reverence until we find time to contemplate God's holiness; and I do not know any place that will lead us to such a fruitful contemplation of God's holiness as when we take our place near the cross. "We preach Christ crucified," because the preaching of the doctrine helps us create and preserve a sense of the holiness of our God.

Christ crucified reveals the awfulness of sin. We preach Christ crucified, because it is the doctrine that incomparably creates and preserves the sense of the nature of sin. Any doctrine that unveils the holiness of God reveals also the horribleness of sin; any doctrine that obscures God's holiness veneers man's sin. If God were merely the easy-going, good-natured, lax, and kindly Deity of many modern worshipers, sin would remain for ever essentially unrevealed. God the lax, the kindly, good-natured, easy-going, would just bend over His rebellious children and say, "My children, I forgive you." Well, my brethren, that might make us easy, but it would never make us good.

Forgiveness is counterfeit when it decorates the sin it forgives. Such forgiveness only paves the way for a repetition of the offense. All true forgiveness throws a most lurid illumination on the sin that is forgiven. That is true in purely human relations. A father's forgiveness is criminal if it benumbs the consciousness of the crime. If, when I forgive my child, my forgiveness diminishes his sense of sin, then I become a participant in the sin I forgive. That is the thoughtless, easy-going, good-natured goodness of the world to which our Master solemnly refers when He says, "If any man love child more than Me, he cannot be My disciple" (see Luke 14:26, 27; Matthew 10:37). If any man love his child in such a way as to make his child more Christless, if he love his child in such a way as to gloss over his young one's sin, then I say his very tenderness and his very forgiveness will appear hateful in the sight of God, for his tenderness and his forgiveness have made sin appear to be less hateful and less revolting, and he can have none of the spirit of the Master and be none of His.

In the light of all true forgiveness, sin is revealed to be as black as the nether hell. Where, then, shall I see the horrors of sin? Where forgiveness is most truly revealed. Where shall I see sin most keenly? Where forgiveness is supremely revealed. In the place of forgiveness I shall see the unutterable horrors of sin.

Well, then, I turn to the Sermon on the Mount. I find no awakening there. I find great prinicples, lofty ideals, severe standards, great moral maxims. I bask in the soft sunny inspiration of great encouragements; I tremble amid the lightning flashes of appalling warnings; my incompletenesses yawn before me; all my defects are ragged and jagged in the burning noon, but I do not feel ashamed of the pain and the horribleness and the fearfulness of sin. It is not otherwise when I turn even to the story of the prodigal son. I may be melted into tears, and yet my tears may not help my vision. Many a man has been made homesick by the story of the prodigal who has nevertheless not been made sick of his sin. What I want is something that will not merely make me homesick, but something that will reveal to me the hatefulness of sin, the leprous disgustingness of sin, that I may not only turn away home, but recoil from sin in contempt as a healthy man turns from diseased and disgusting food. That is what I want. And I do not see or fear my sin in the Sermon on the Mount. Nor do I fear and find it in the story of the prodigal son.

But when I stand at the cross; when I lift my eyes to the crucified Son of God; when I recall the word that He spoke, "God so loved the world that He gave His Son" (John 3:16), in the love that blazes in that death I can see something of the sin for which He died. I see it, as I see it nowhere else. When I stand at the cross, I am permitted in my measure to see sin through the eyes of my God. The cross is the place of great awakening for sinners. And explain it as we may, or leave it unexplained, the experience of the Christian church has gathered abundant witness to the truth of this statement. It is in the place where forgiveness is most supremely revealed that men have gained the most searching convictions of their sin.

It has been always at the preaching of the cross that men have been pricked—we have not a better word yet—that men have been pricked in their heart. Just look at the old apostolic word. They were, says the

Acts of the Apostles, "pricked in their heart" (2:37), pricked, goaded, irritated. First they were made irritable and filled with unrest until it touched the heart and became a pain and an agony. Nowhere else, nohow else, can you get the pain and the shame and the fear of sin which you find awakened at the cross. And if we men and women of this latter day wish to gaze into the awfulness of sin, we shall have to take our stand at the mystic confluence of midnight and noonday and abide in the cross of our Lord Jesus Christ. "In Thy light shall we see light," and part of the illumination will be the veritable horror of sin.

Christ crucified demonstrates grace. We preach Christ crucified, because it is a doctrine in the experience of which we incomparably discern the realities of grace. The cross is not merely the birthplace of my fears, or the birthplace of my shames, or the birthplace of my disgusts. It is the birthplace of the radiant and immortal hope. I like old John Nelson's words when he was preaching about the influence of John Wesley's preaching and its effect upon him. When he had done, he said, "This man can tell the secrets of my heart, but he has not left me there, he has showed me the remedy, even the blood of Christ. Then was my soul filled with consolation, through hope that God, for Christ's sake, would save me." But that has not been merely the experience of John Nelson: it has been the experience wherever Christ, and Him crucified, has been proclaimed.

Where has the sanctified comfort of the Christian church been found? Not far from the cross! "And I say in my dream that just as Christian came up to the cross his burden loosed from off his shoulders and fell from off his back, and began to tumble, and so continued to do until it came to the mouth of the sepulcher, where it fell in, and I saw it no more. Then was Christian glad and lightsome, and said with a moving heart, 'He has given me rest by His sorrow and life by His death!'" But I will turn away from John Bunyan, who might be thought to be a very partial witness to the power of his

Lord, and I will turn to a little frequented path, to Goethe, perhaps to Goethe's masterpiece. Let me give you just a short extract from those wonderful words in the *Confessions of a Beautiful Soul:*

"I leaned on a little table beside me and I hid my tear-stained face in my hands, and who could ever express even in the dimmest way the experience that came to me then? A secret influence drew my soul to the cross where Jesus once expired. It was an inward leaning—I cannot give it any other name—an inward leaning like that which draws the heart to its beloved in its absence. As my soul drew near to Him who became mine and died upon the cross, in that moment I knew what faith meant, and in that moment my spirit received a wholly new power of uplifting." Worthy perhaps to stand side by side with the testimony of John Bunyan!

But one need not go to literature for one's instances to prove that it is just at the cross men lose their burden and find the truth of the realities of grace. A very dear and intimate friend of mine only this last week related to me a dream that had been blessed by God to the redemption of his own father. The father dreamed that he was a hare, and a hare he was. So real and so graphic was the consciousness of the dream that he felt he could almost smell the dewy turnip-tops of the fields amongst which he moved. Suddenly he heard the cry of the hounds. He pricked his ears, listened, and bolted full pace across the fields. The hounds drew nearer and nearer, and came at last so close to him that he could feel their hot breath. Then he found that he was leaving the green pastures and was reaching bare and rugged heights, and just when he had reached those bare and rocky heights he became conscious that his pursuers were not hounds. They were his sins, and he was a flying soul! Away up, away up, away up towards the summit he saw a cave, and terrified beyond measure he made for the cave and then turned round. The entrance to the cave was flooded with a most unearthly light, and just in the center of the opening there shone resplendently a cross, standing between him and the awful things that pursues. He awoke, and behold, it was a dream. But by the power of the dream he was redeemed.

Rock of Ages, cleft for me,
Let me hide myself in Thee.

Christ crucified gives us spiritual health. We preach Christ crucified because it is the doctrine in whose heart we find ample resources for the attainment of moral and spiritual health. It is not merely a kindly friend who comes and gives you the gratifications of a pleasant and fleeting sentiment. The doctrine of Christ, and Him crucified, is generative of moral and spiritual force. It is the doctrine above all others, so far as my experience in the ministry can tell, which is productive of the ethical life. It is the power of God unto salvation. I think I can almost feel the thrill of the apostle Paul's heart when he said it: The gospel of God is "the power of God unto salvation" (Romans 1:16), right up to it, not merely to regeneration, but to sanctification and perfect health. It is the power of God until God Himself shall put His hand upon me and say, "Saved!" It is the daily foes, to front them in confidence, to overcome them, not faintingly, but to be more than a conqueror, to march over them as a man in Christ my God.

So I say that for ethical revivals we must first of all have evangelical revivals. We must first of all have the doctrine of the cross before we can hope for moral elevation. I wonder how many of my audience have read David Brainerd's *Journal of His Life and Doings Amongst the North American Indians?* If my young brethren in the ministry would take a word from me, they would buy that book and have it by the bedside. Next to John Wesley's *Journal* it is the book in which I find most devotional help. Get David Brainerd's *Life and Journal*, edited by Jonathan Edwards, and turn to the end, where you will find an essay by David Brainerd on the doctrine he preached among the Indians, where he makes a statement that is full of heartening to myself in my own ministry. He says, "I never got away from Jesus, and Him crucified, and I found that when my people were gripped by this great evangelical doctrine of Christ, and Him crucified, I had no need to give them instructions about morality. I found that one followed as the sure and inevitable fruit of the other." That is a wonderful word to come from a saintly man like David Brainerd, who hated sin as he feared hell! He said, "I find my Indians begin to put on the garments of holiness, and their common life begins to be sanctified even in a trifle when they are possessed by the doctrine of Christ, and Him crucified." When I look round among my people, and look round in my nation, and long for an ethical revival for the reformation of outward manners and life, I know that the power in which it is to be accomplished is the preaching of Christ, and Him crucified. Christ, and Him crucified, is the doctrine which is to be captive of the moral reformation of our country.

How Do We Preach Christ Crucified?

How is a great gospel like this to be preached? If it is the doctrine in which I best discern the holiness of God, if it is the doctrine in which I discover the horribleness of sin, if it is the doctrine which reveals to me the realities of grace, if it is the doctrine in which I find the resources of ethical revival—How shall I preach it? There is only one way. *A gospel of infinite compassion must be preached in the spirit of compassion in which it was born.* My brethren in the ministry, we need to pray, and to pray long and to pray fervently, that we may never become hard. I think if there is one thing we need more than another it is the grace of compassion. We want to have a spirit of compassion until we almost instinctively perceive the poignant need of those to whom we seek to minister.

I have gone more than once in my ministry in Newcastle and got as near as I could to the place on which John Wesley stood when he preached his first sermon among the Northumbrians. I dare say you remember that part of his *Journal* where he says that he thinks he had never noticed such wickedness as he encountered in Newcastle-on-Tyne, such blasphemy, such cursing, such swearing even from the mouths of little children. I always read the *Journal* there with great and tender interest, because I wondered how John Wesley would think and feel in face of such a horrible state of things. You know he just adds in his *Journal*, "Surely this place is ripe for the Master."* I do not think you will be surprised to learn that preaching to those undone and diseased folk of Northumbria he took one of the tenderest texts he could find, and preached on "He was wounded for our transgressions; He was bruised for our iniquities" (Isaiah 53:5). And then he tells us in the very next paragraph that when he had done, the people just clung to his clothes and to his hands. He had brought them to the Master and to the cross.

It is the same power today. Our God is willing to be powerful, willing to manifest an energy which shall compel men to stand, to wonder, and to pray, not only here but in all lands. It is the power of God unto salvation. If we are to retain, or even to gain, this spirit of compassion, we ourselves must live very near the cross; and abiding by the cross, it is possible for us to be bathed in the compassions that fail not; and with the message upon our lips of Christ, and Him crucified, we shall gather many souls unto God.

---

* John Wesley, *The Heart of Wesley's Journal* (Grand Rapids: Kregel Publications, 1989), p. 85.

NOTES

The Offense of the Cross

George H. Morrison (1866-1928) assisted the great Alexander Whyte in Edinburgh, pastored two churches, and then became a pastor in 1902 of the distinguished Wellington Church on University Avenue in Glasgow. His preaching drew great crowds; in fact, people had to line up an hour before the services to be sure to get seats in the large auditorium. Morrison was a master of imagination in preaching, yet his messages were solidly biblical.

From his many published volumes of sermons, I have chosen this message, found in *The Wings of the Morning*, published by Hodder and Stoughton, London.

George H. Morrison

4

THE OFFENSE OF THE CROSS

Then is the offence of the cross ceased (Galatians 5:11).

ONE THING THAT marks the ministry of Paul is how he lovingly yearned over the Jews. With a quenchless and intense desire, he prayed that they might be brought into the fold. Never a did mother so long for the saving of her son as Paul longed for the saving of his countrymen. He was willing to suffer anything or everything, if only his people Israel might be won.

It is when we remember that deep longing that we realize what the cross meant for Paul. For the great stumbling block for the Jews—the offense that made the gospel of Christ smell rank to them—was, as our text indicates, the cross. Take that away, and it would be a thousand times more easy to win the Jews to the acceptance of the Lord. Say nothing about that, just slur it over, and you would take half the difficulty out of the way of Israel. Yet, in spite of his yearning to see Israel saved, that was the one theme Paul would not ignore. God forbid, he says, that I should glory save in the cross of Jesus Christ my Lord.

There is a great lesson there for Christian teachers, and for all who are trying to advance Christ's kingdom. The more earnest and eager they are to have men saved, the more willing they are to go all lengths to meet them. And that is right, for we must be all things to all men—to the Jews as a Jew, to the Romans as a Roman; but remember, there are a few great facts we cannot yield, though they run counter to the whole spirit of the age. It were better to empty a church and preach the cross, than to fill it by keeping silent like a coward. It were better to fail as Paul failed with the Jews, than to succeed by being a traitor to the cross.

And that is why I look with such uncertainty on much that the church is trying to do today. Religion can never be a pleasant entertainment. When the offense of the cross ceases, it is lost.

Why Is the Cross an Offense?

Now I want tonight to make a little plainer to you why the cross was an offense to the Jews, and to put things in such a way that you may see at once that the same causes are operative still.

The cross was offensive to the Jews just because it blighted all their hopes. It shattered every dream they ever dreamed, every ideal that ever glimmered on them. No telegram of news full of disaster, plunging a man into unlooked-for poverty—no sudden death of one whom the heart clings to, laying a man's life in ruins at his feet—nothing could more certainly shatter a man's hopes than did the cross shatter the vision of the Jews. They had prayed for and had dreamed of their Messiah, and he was to come in power as a conqueror. "Prepare ye the way of the Lord, make His paths straight" (Matthew 3:3)—you can almost hear the tramp of victorious feet. That was the light which burned in the Jewish darkness; that was the song which made music in their hearts. Then in the place of the triumph, there comes Calvary. In place of the Christ victorious, comes Christ crucified. And was this the Messiah who was to trample Rome, pierced in hands and feet by Roman nails? To the Jews a stumbling block: you cannot wonder at it, when every hope they had formed was contradicted. Yet, in spite of it all, Paul preached Christ crucified, and that was the offense of the cross.

Now I venture to say that that offense of Calvary is just as powerful now as it was then. If I know anything about the ideals men cherish now, and about the hopes that reign in ten thousand hearts, they are as antagonistic to the cross as was the Jewish ideal of Messiah. Written across Calvary is sacrifice; written across this age of ours is pleasure. On the lips of Christ are the stern words, I must die. On the lips of this age of ours, I must enjoy. When I think of the passion to be rich and the judgment of everything by money standards, of the feverish desire at all costs to be happy, of the frivolity, of the worship of success; and then contrast it with the "pale and solemn scene" upon the hill, I know that the offense of Calvary is not ceased. Unto the Jews a stumbling block—unto far more than the Jews: unto a pleasure-loving world and a dead church. Therefore say nothing about it. Let it be. Make everything interesting, pleasant, easy. Then is the offense of the cross ceased—and with it the power of the gospel.

Once more, *the cross was an offense to the Jews because it swept away much that they took a pride in.* If there was any meaning in Calvary at all, some of their most cherished things were valueless. The Jews were preeminently a religious people, and this is always one peril of religious people. It is to take the things that lead to God and let the heart grow centered upon them. There was the ceremonial law for instance, with its scrupulous abhorrence of defilements. No one who has not studied the whole matter can ever know what that meant to the Jew. And there were the sacrifices smoking upon their altars, and the feasts and festivals and journeys to Jerusalem. And there was the Temple, that magnificent building—a sign of their hope and symbol of their unity. At least let this be said of that old people, that if they were proud, they were proud of worthy things. It is better to be proud of law and temple than to be proud of battleship and millionaire. Yet all that pride, religious though it was—that pride, deep-rooted as the people's life—all that was swept away like autumn leaves if there was any meaning in the cross. No more would the eyes of men turn to Jerusalem, no more would sacrifices fill the altars, no more was there room for ceremonial law if the Son of God had died upon the tree. And it was this crushing into the very dust of all that was dearest to the Jewish heart that was so bitter an offense of Calvary.

Today, has that offense of the cross ceased? Has that stumbling block been removed? I say that this is still the offense of Calvary, that it cuts at the root of so much that we are proud of. Here is a woman who strives to do her duty. God bless her, she does it very bravely. Here is a student proud of his high gifts. God prosper him that he may use them well. But over against reliance upon duty and all attempts of the reason to give peace, there hangs the crucified Redeemer saying, "No man cometh unto the Father but by Me" (John 14:6). Here is the offense of the cross in cultured ages. It is that a man must come with empty hands. He must come as one who knows his utter need of the pardoning mercy of Almighty God. In an age like ours—one that leans upon its heritage and is proud of its magnificent achievement—that call to unconditional surrender is the offense of evangelical religion. We are all tempted to despise what we get freely. We like a little toil and sweat and travail. We measure the value of most things not by their own worth, but by all that it has cost us to procure them. And Calvary costs us nothing though it cost God everything. The love and the life of it are freely offered, and to a commercial age and a commercial city there is something suspicious and offensive there. Ah sirs, if I preached salvation by good works what an appreciative audience I could have! How it would appeal to many an eager heart in the young and teeming life of this great city! But I trample that temptation under foot— not that I love you less but that I love Christ more. I pray that here, where the gospel is proclaimed, the offense of the cross of Christ may never cease. I do not believe that if you scratch a man you will find underneath his skin a Christian. I do not believe that if you do your best all is well for time and for eternity. But I do believe—

Not the labors of my hands
Can fulfil Thy law's demands;
Could my zeal no respite know,

Could my tears for ever flow,
All for sin could not atone:
Thou must save, and Thou alone.

The cross was an offense to the Jews because it obliterated national distinctions. It leveled at one blow those social barriers that were of such untold worth in Jewish eyes. It was supremely important that the Jews should stand apart; through their isolation God had educated them. They had had the bittersweet privilege of being lonely, and being lonely they had been ennobled. Unto them were committed the oracles of God; they were a chosen nation, a peculiar people. The covenants were theirs, theirs were the promises. The knowledge of the one true God was theirs until at last, almost inevitably, there rose in the Jewish mind a certain separateness, and a certain contempt, continually deepening, for all the other nations of mankind. They had no envy of the art of Greece. They were not awed by the majesty of Rome. Grecians and Romans, Persians and Assyrians—powerful, cultured, victorious—were but Gentiles. There is something almost sublime in the contempt with which that little nation viewed the world. Then came the cross. It leveled all distinctions; it burst through all barriers of nationality. There was neither Jew nor Gentile, Greek nor barbarian, but Christ was all and in all. Let some wild savage from the farthest west come to the cross of Christ pleading for mercy, and he had nothing less to do, and nothing more, than the proudest Jew who was a child of Abraham. One feels in an instant the insult of it all; how it left the Jew defenseless in the wild. All he had clung to was gone; his vineyard-wall was shattered; he must live or die now in the wind-swept world. And this tremendous leveling of distinctions—this striking out Jew and writing in humanity—this, to the proud, reserved, and lonely people, was no small part of the offense of Calvary.

Now, I would not have you imagine for a moment that Christ disregards all personal distinctions. If I sent you away harboring the thought that all who come

to Christ get the same treatment, I should have done
Him an unutterable wrong. In everything He did Christ
was original, because He was fresh from God into the
world. Yet in no sphere was He so strikingly original
as in the way He handled those who came to Him. So
was it when He was on the earth: so is it now when He
is hid with God. There is always some touch, some
word, some discipline that tells of an individual
understanding. But in spite of all that, and recognizing
that, I say that this is the "scandal" of the cross, that
there every distinction is obliterated, and men must be
saved as lost or not at all.

You remember the lady from a gentle home who
went to hear the preaching of George Whitefield? She
listened in disgust to a great sermon and then, like
Naaman, went away in a rage. "For it is perfectly
intolerable," she said, "that ladies like me should be
spoken to just like a creature from the streets." Quite
so: it is perfectly intolerable—and that is the stumbling
block of Calvary. Are you, who may be cultured to your
fingertips, to be classed with the savage who cannot
read or write? It would be very pleasant to say "No"—
but then the offense of the cross would be removed.

A friend of mine who is a busy doctor in a thriving
borough not 10 miles from Glasgow was called in the
other day to see a patient who, as was plain at the first
glance, was dying. The doctor, a good Christian, said,
"Friend, the best service I can do you is to ask, Have
you made your peace with God?" Whereon the man,
raising his wasted arm, and piercing the questioner
with awe-filled eyes, said, "Doctor, is it as bad as that?"
I want to say it is always as bad as that. I want to say
it to the brightest heart here. You do need pardon and
peace with God in Christ as much as the wildest
prodigal in Glasgow. Accept it. It is freely offered you.
Say, "Thou, O Christ, art all I want." And then, just as
the wilderness will blossom, so will the offense of the
cross become its glory.

NOTES

The Death of Christ for His People

Charles Haddon Spurgeon (1834-1892) is undoubtedly the most famous minister of modern times. Converted in 1850, he united with the Baptists and soon began to preach in various places. He became pastor of the Baptist church in Waterbeach in 1851, and three years later he was called to the decaying Park Street Church, London. Within a short time, the work began to prosper, a new church was built and dedicated in 1861, and Spurgeon became London's most popular preacher. In 1855, he began to publish his sermons weekly; and today they make up the fifty-seven volumes of *The Metropolitan Tabernacle Pulpit*. He founded a pastor's college and several orphanages.

This sermon is taken from *The Metropolitan Tabernacle Pulpit*, volume 46. It was preached by Spurgeon in 1857.

Charles Haddon Spurgeon

5

THE DEATH OF CHRIST
FOR HIS PEOPLE

He laid down his life for us (1 John 3:16).

COME, BELIEVER, AND contemplate this sublime truth, thus proclaimed to thee in simple monosyllables: "He laid down his life for us." There is not one long word in the sentence; it is all as simple as it can be; and it is simple because it is sublime. Sublimity in thought always needs simplicity in words to express itself. Little thoughts require great words to explain them; little preachers need Latin words to convey their feeble ideas, but great thoughts and great expressers of those thoughts are content with little words.

"He laid down his life for us." Here there is not much upon which any man can display his eloquence. Here is little room for metaphysical discussion or for deep thought. The text sets before us a simple yet sublime doctrine. What, then, shall I do with it? If I would speak of it profitably to myself, since I need not employ my wit to dissect it, nor my oratory to proclaim it, let me exercise my adoration to worship it. Let me prostrate all my powers before the throne, and, like an angel when his work is done, and he has nowhere else to fly at his Lord's command, let me fold the wings of my contemplation and stand before the throne of this great truth. Let me meekly bow myself and worship Him that was, and is, and is to come—the great and glorious One who "laid down his life for us."

It will be well for me, in commencing my discourse, to remind you that there is no understanding the death of Christ unless we understand the person of Christ. If I were to tell you that God died for us, although I might be telling you a truth, and you might possibly not misunderstand what I meant, yet I should be at the same time uttering an error. God cannot die. It is, of course, impossible, from His very nature, that he could even for a moment cease to exist. God is incapable of suffering. It is true that we sometimes use words to express emotions on the part of God, but we speak after the manner of men. He is impassive. He cannot suffer. It is not possible for Him to endure aught; much less, then, is it possible for him to suffer death. Yet we are told, in the verse from which our text is taken, "Hereby perceive we the love *of God.*" You notice that the words *of God* are inserted by the translators. They are in italics because they are not in the original. A better translation would be, "Hereby perceive we love." But when we read "of God," it might lead the ignorant to fancy that God could die; whereas, God could not. We must always understand, and constantly remember, that our Lord Jesus Christ was "very God of very God," and that, as God, He had all the attributes of the Most High, and could not, therefore, be capable either of suffering or death. But then He was also man, "man of the substance of his mother," man, just like ourselves, sin alone excepted. And the Lord Jesus dies not as God; it was as man that he gave up the ghost; as man, He was nailed to the cross. As God, He was in heaven, even when His body was in the tomb. As God, He was swaying the scepter of all worlds even when the mock scepter of reed was in His hand, and the imperial robe of universal monarchy was on the eternal shoulders of His Godhead when the soldier's old purple cloak was wrapped about His manhood. He did not cease to be God. He did not lose his omnipotence and His eternal dominion when He became man; nor did He, as God, die or suffer. It was as man that He "laid down his life for us."

Three Lessons From Christ's Sacrifice

Come, now, my soul, and worship this man, this God. Come, believer, and behold thy Savior. Come to the innermost circle of all sanctity, the circle that contains the cross of Christ, and here sit down. And, while you worship, learn three lessons from the fact that "he laid down his life for us." The first lesson should be, Did He lay down His life for us? Ah! then, my brethren, how great must have been our sins that they could not have been atoned for at any other price! Second, did He lay down His life for us? Ah! then, beloved, how great must have been His love! He would not stop short anywhere, until life itself had been resigned. Third, did He lay down His life for us? Ah! then, my soul, be of good cheer; how safe art thou! If such an atonement has been offered, if such a sure satisfaction has been given to Almighty God, how secure thou art! Who can destroy him who has been bought with the blood of such a Redeemer?

How great must have been my sins, *if Christ lay down his life for me? Come, then, let me believingly meditate on this first sad fact.*

Ah! my brethren, I will speak a little of my own experience, and in so doing I shall also be describing yours. I have seen my sins in many different ways. I saw them once by the blazing light of Sinai; and, oh! my spirit shrank within me, for my sins seemed exceeding black. When the sound of the trumpet waxed loud and long, and the lightning and fire flashed into my heart, I saw a very hell of iniquity within my soul, and I was ready then to curse the day that I was born, that I should have had such a heart, so vile and so deceitful. I thought that then I had seen the exceeding blackness of my sin. Alas! I had not seen enough of sin to make me loathe it so as to leave it, for that conviction passed away. Sinai was but a volcano, and it was hushed to silence; and then I began to play with sin again, and loved it as much as ever.

I beheld another sight one day; I saw my sins by the light of heaven. I looked up, and I considered the heavens, the work of God's fingers. I perceived the purity of God's character written on the sunbeams, I saw His holiness engraved upon the wide world, as well as revealed in Scripture; and as I compared myself with Him, I thought I saw how black I was. O God! I never knew the heinousness of my own guilt until I saw the glory of Thy character. But now I see the brightness of Thy holiness, my whole soul is cast down at the thought of my sinfulness, and my great departure from the living God. I thought that, then, I had seen enough. Ah! I had seen enough to make me worship for a moment; but my gladness was as the early cloud and as the morning dew, and I went my way, and forgot what manner of man I was. When I had lost the sense of the majesty of God, I lost also the consciousness of my own guilt.

Then there came to me another view, and I beheld God's loving kindness to me. I saw how He had dandled me upon the knee of Providence—how he had carried me all my life long and had strewn my path with plenty, giving me all things richly to enjoy. I remembered how He had been with me in the hour of trial, how He had preserved me in the day of hurricane, and kept me safe at the moment of storm. I remembered all His goodness to me; and, struck with surprise at His mercy, I looked upon my sin in the light of His grace; and I said, "O sin, how base thou art, what dire ingratitude dost thou manifest against a God so profoundly kind!"

I thought, then, surely I had seen the worst of sin, when I had laid it side by side, first with the character of God, and afterwards with his bounties. I cursed sin from my inmost heart, and thought I had seen enough of it. But, ah! my brethren, I had not. That sense of gratitude passed away, and I found myself still prone to sin, and still loving it.

But, oh, there came a thrice-happy, yet thrice-mournful hour! One day, in my wanderings, I heard a cry, a groan; methought 'twas not a cry such as came from mortal lip, it had in it such unutterable depths of wondrous woe. I turned aside, expecting to see some great sight; and it was indeed a great sight that I saw. Lo, there, upon a tree, all bleeding, hung a man. I marked the misery that made His flesh all quiver on

His bones. I beheld the dark clouds come rolling down from heaven, like the chariots of misery. I saw them clothe His brow with blackness; I saw even in the thick darkness, for mine eyes were opened, and I perceived that His heart was as full of the gloom and horror of grief as the sky was full of blackness. Then I seemed to look into His soul, and I saw there torrents of unutterable anguish—wells of torment of such an awful character that mortal lip dare not sip, lest it should be burned with scalding heat. I said, "Who is this mighty sufferer? Why doth He suffer thus? Has He been the greatest of all sinners, the basest of all blasphemers?" But a voice came forth from the excellent glory, and it said, "This is My beloved Son; but He took the sinner's sin upon himself, and He must bear its penalty." O God! I thought, I never saw sin till that hour, when I saw it tear Christ's glories from His head, when it seemed for a moment even to withdraw the lovingkindness of God from Him, when I saw Him covered with His own blood, and plunged into the uttermost depths of oceans of grief. Then I said, "Now shall I know what thou art, O sin, as never before I knew it!" Though those other sights might teach me something of the dire character of evil, yet never, till I saw the Savior on the tree, did I understand how base a traitor man's guilt was to man's God.

O heir of heaven, lift now thine eye, and behold the scenes of suffering through which thy Lord passed for thy sake! Come in the moonlight, and stand between those olives; see Him sweat great drops of blood. Go from that garden, and follow to Pilate's bar. See your Master subjected to the grossest and filthiest insult; gaze upon the face of spotless beauty defiled with the spittle of soldiers; see His head pierced with thorns; mark His back, all rent, and torn, and scarred, and bruised, and bleeding beneath the terrible lash. And O Christian, see Him die! Go and stand where His mother stood, and hear Him say to thee, "Man, behold thy Savior!" Come thou tonight, and stand where John stood; hear Him cry, "I thirst," and find thyself unable either to assuage His griefs or to comprehend their bitterness. Then, when thou hast wept there, lift thine hand, and cry, "Revenge!" Bring out the traitors; where are they? And when your sins are brought forth as the murderers of Christ, let no death be too painful for them; though it should involve the cutting off of right arms, or the quenching of right eyes, and putting out their light forever; do it! For if these murderers murdered Christ, then let them die. Die terribly they may, but die they must. Oh! that God the Holy Spirit would teach you that first lesson, my brethren, the boundless wickedness of sin, for Christ had to lay down his life before your sin could be wiped away.

How greatly He must have loved me. Now we will come to the second head, and here we will lift up our hearts from the depths of sadness to the heights of affection. Did the Savior lay down His life for me? We will read it now, "He laid down his life for me;" and I pray the Lord to help each of you, by faith, to read it so, because, when we say "us," that is dealing in generalities—blessed generalities, it is true—but let us, at this time, deal in specialities, and say, each one of us who can do so truthfully, "He laid down his life for me." Yes, HOW GREATLY HE MUST HAVE LOVED ME!

Ah, Lord Jesus! I never knew Thy love till I understood the meaning of Thy death. Beloved, we shall try again, if we can, to tell the story of our own experience, to let you see how God's love is to be learned. Come, saint, sit down, and meditate on thy creation. Note how marvelously thou hast been formed, and how all thy bones are fitted to one another, and see love there. Next, notice the predestination which placed thee where thou art; for the lines have fallen unto thee in pleasant places. Notwithstanding all thy troubles, thou hast, compared with many a poor soul, "a goodly heritage." Notice, then, the love of God displayed in the predestination that has made thee what thou art, and placed thee where thou art. Then look thou back, and see the lovingkindness of thy Lord, as displayed to thee in all thy journey up till now. Thou art getting old, and thy hair is whitening above thy brow; but He has carried thee all the days of old; not one good thing has failed of all that the Lord thy God has promised. Recall thy life story. Go back now, and look at the tapestry of thy life, which God has been working every day with the golden filament of His love, and see what pictures of grace there are upon it. Canst thou not say that Jesus has loved thee? Turn thine eye back, and read the ancient rolls of the everlasting covenant, and see thy name amongst the first-born, the elect, the church of the living God. Say, did He not love thee when He wrote thy name there? Go and remember how the eternal settlements were made, and how God decreed and arranged all things so that thy salvation should come to pass. Say, was there not love there?

Pause at the remembrance of thy convictions; think of thy conversion; recollect thy preservation, and how God's grace has been working upon thee, in adoption, in justification, and in every item of the new covenant. When thou hast summed up all these things, let me ask thee this question: Do all these things produce in thee such a sense of gratitude as the one thing that I shall mention now, the cross of our Lord Jesus Christ? For, my brother, if thy mind is like mine, although thou wilt think highly enough of all these things that God has given thee, thou wilt be obliged to confess that the thought of the death of Christ upon the cross swallows them all up. This I know, my brethren: I may look back, I may look forward, but whether I look back to the decrees of eternity or look forward to the pearl-gated city and all the splendors that God has prepared for his own beloved children, I can never see my Father's love so beaming forth, in all its radiant splendor, as when I look at the cross of Christ, and see Him die thereon. I can read the love of God in the rocky letters of the eternal covenant, and in the blazing letters of heaven hereafter; but, my brethren, in those crimson lines, those lines written in blood, there is something more striking than there is anywhere else, for they say, "He laid down his life for us." Ah, here it is ye learn love.

You know the old story of Damon and Pythias—how the two friends struggled together as to which should die for the other; there was love there. But, ah! there is no comparison between Damon and Pythias, and a poor sinner and his Savior. Christ laid down His life, His glorious life, for a poor worm. He stripped Himself of all His splendors, then of all His happiness, then of His own righteousness, then of His own robes, till He was naked to His own shame. Then He laid down His life, that was all He had left, for our Savior had not kept anything back.

Just think of that for a moment. He had a crown in heaven; but he laid that aside so you and I might wear one forever. He had a girdle of brightness—brighter than the stars—about His loins; but He took it off and laid it by so you and I might eternally wear a girdle of righteousness. He had listened to the holy songs of the cherubim and seraphim, but He left them all that we might forever dwell where angels sing. Then He came to earth, and He had many things, even in His poverty, which might have tended to his comfort. He laid down first one glory, and then another, at love's demand. At last, it came to this: He had nothing left but one poor garment, woven from the top throughout and clinging to His back with blood, and He laid down that also. Then there was nothing left. He had not kept back one single thing. "There," He might have said, "take an inventory of all I have, to the last farthing; I have given it all up for My people's ransom." And there was nothing left now but His own life. O love insatiable! Couldst thou not stay there? He had given up one hand to cancel sin and the other hand to reconcile us unto God. He had given up one foot that we might have our sinful feet forever transfixed, and nailed, and fastened, ne'er to wander, and the other foot to be fastened to the tree that we might have our feet at liberty to run the heavenly race. There was nothing left but His poor heart, and He gave His heart up too. They set it abroach with the spear, and forthwith there came out blood and water.

Ah, my Lord! what have I ever given to Thee compared to what Thou hast given for me? Some poor things, like some rusty farthings, I have given Thee—but how little compared with what Thou hast given me! Now and then, my Lord, I have given Thee a poor song upon an ill-toned instrument. Sometimes, my Lord, I have done some little service for Thee; but, alas! my fingers were so black they spoiled what I intended to have presented to Thee white as snow. I have done nothing for Thee, my Lord. No, though I have been a missionary and surrendered home and friends; no, though I have been a martyr, and given my body to be burned, I will say, in the last hour, "My Master, I have done nothing for Thee, after all, in comparison with what Thou hast done for me; and yet, what can I do more? How can I show my love to Thee, for Thy love to me, so peerless, so matchless? What shall I do? I will do nothing but—

> Dissolved by thy goodness, I'll fall to the ground,
> And weep to the praise of the mercy I've found.
> That is all I can do, and that I must and will do.

How safe I am. Now, beloved, we will change the theme, and go one note higher. We have run up the gamut a long way, and now we have just reached the height of the octave. But we have something else to get out of the text: "He laid down his life for us." Did my Savior lay down his life for me? Then, HOW SAFE I AM!

We will have no controversy tonight with those who do not see this truth; the Lord open their blind eyes and show it to them! That is all we will say. We who know the gospel see in the fact of the death of Christ a reason that no strength of logic can ever shake, and no power of unbelief can remove, why we should be saved. There may be men with minds so distorted that they can conceive it possible that Christ should die for a man who afterwards is lost; I say, there may be such. I am sorry to say that there are still to be found some such persons, whose brains have been so addled in their childhood that they cannot see what they hold is both a preposterous falsehood and a blasphemous libel. Christ dies for a man, and then God punishes that man again; Christ suffers in a sinner's stead, and then God condemns that sinner after all! Why, my friends, I feel quite shocked in only mentioning such an awful error. Were it not so current as it is, I should certainly pass it over with the contempt that it deserves.

The doctrine of holy Scripture is this, that God is just, that Christ died in the stead of His people, and that, as God is just, He will never punish one solitary soul of Adam's race for whom the Savior did thus shed His blood. The Savior did, indeed, in a certain sense, die for all; all men receive many a mercy through His blood. But that He was the substitute and surety for all men is so inconsistent, both with reason and Scripture, that we are obliged to reject the doctrine with abhorrence. No, my soul, how shalt thou be punished if thy Lord endured thy punishment for thee? Did He die for thee? O my soul, if Jesus was not thy substitute and did not die in thy very stead, then He is no Savior to thee! But if He was thy substitute, if He suffered as thy surety, in thy stead, then, my soul, "Who is he that condemneth?" Christ has died, yea, rather, has risen again, and sitteth at the right hand of God, and maketh intercession for us. There stands the master-argument: Christ "laid down his life for us," and "if, when we were enemies, we were reconciled to God saved by his life" (Romans 5:10). If the agonies of the Savior put our sins away, the everlasting life of the Savior, with the merits of His death added thereunto, must preserve His people, even unto the end.

This much I know—ye may hear men stammer when they say it—but what I preach is the old Lutheran, Calvinistic, Augustinian, Pauline, Christian truth: There is not one sin in the Book of God against anyone that believeth. Our sins were numbered on the

Scapegoat's head, and there is not one sin that ever a believer did commit that has any power to damn him, for Christ has taken the damning power out of sin, by allowing it, to speak by a bold metaphor, to damn Himself, for sin did condemn Him. Inasmuch as sin condemned Him, sin cannot condemn us. O believer, this is thy security, that all thy sin and guilt, all thy transgressions and thine iniquities, have been atoned for, and were atoned for before they were committed. Thou mayest come with boldness, though red with all crimes and black with every lust, and lay thine hand on that Scapegoat's head. When thou hast put thine hand there and seen that Scapegoat driven into the wilderness, thou mayest clap thine hands for joy, and say, "It is finished, sin is pardoned."

> Here's pardon for transgressions past,
> It matters not how black their cast;
> And oh, my soul, with wonder view,
> For sins to come, here's pardon too!

This is all I want to know: Did the Savior die for me? Then I will not continue in sin that grace may abound. Nothing shall stop me of thus glorying, in all the churches of the Lord Jesus, that my sins are entirely removed from me; and, in God's sight, I may sing, as Hart did sing,—

> With Christ's spotless vesture on,
> Holy as the Holy One.

O marvelous death of Christ, how securely dost thou set the feet of God's people on the rocks of eternal love; and how securely dost thou keep them there! Come, dear brethren, let us suck a little honey out of this honeycomb. Was there ever anything so luscious and so sweet to the believer's taste as this all-glorious truth that we are complete in Him; that in and through His death and merits we are accepted in the Beloved? Oh, was there ever anything more sublime than this thought, that He has already raised us up together and made us sit together in heavenly places in Christ

Jesus, far above all principalities and powers; just where He sits? Surely there is nothing more sublime than that, except it be that a master-thought stamps all these things with more than their own value—the master-thought that, though the mountains may depart and the hills be removed, the covenant of His love shall never depart from us. "For," saith Jehovah, "I will never forget thee, O Zion; I have graven thee upon the palms of my hands; thy walls are continually before me" (Isaiah 49:14-16). O Christian, that is a firm foundation, cemented with blood, on which thou mayest build for eternity! Ah, my soul! thou needest no other hope but this, Jesus, Thy mercy never dies; I will plead this truth when cast down with anguish—Thy mercy never dies. I will plead this when Satan hurls temptations at me, and when conscience casts the remembrance of my sin in my teeth; I will plead this ever, and I will plead it now:

> Jesus, thy blood and righteousness
> My beauty are, my glorious dress.

Yea, and after I die, and even when I stand before thine eyes, thou dread Supreme:

> When from the dust of death I rise,
> To take my mansion in the skies,
> E'en then shall this be all my plea,
> "Jesus hath lived and died for me."
> Bold shall I stand in that great day,
> For who aught to my charge shall lay?
> While through Christ's blood absolved I am
> From sin's tremendous curse and shame.

Ah, brethren, if this is your experience, you may come to the table of communion now right happily; it will not be coming to a funeral, but to a feast of gladness. "He laid down his life for us."

NOTES

The Cross the Proof of the Love of God

Alexander Maclaren (1826-1910) was one of Great Britain's most famous preachers. While pastoring the Union Chapel, Manchester (1858-1903), he became known as "the prince of expository preachers." Rarely active in denominational or civic affairs, Maclaren invested his time studying the Word in the original and sharing its truths with others in sermons that are still models of effective expository preaching. He published a number of books of sermons and climaxed his ministry by publishing his monumental *Expositions of Holy Scripture.*

This message is taken from *Triumphant Certainties and Other Sermons*, published in 1902 by Funk and Wagnalls.

Alexander Maclaren

6

THE CROSS THE PROOF
OF THE LOVE OF GOD

~~God commendeth His love towards us~~, in that, whilst we were yet sinners, Christ died for us (Romans 5:8).

"GOD COMMENDETH HIS love." That is true and beautiful, but that is not all that the apostle means. We "commend" persons and things when we speak of them with praise and confidence. If that were the meaning of my text, it would represent the death of Christ as setting forth, in a manner to win our hearts, the greatness, the excellence, the transcendency, of God's love. But there is more than that in the words. The expression here employed strictly means "to set two things side by side," and it has two meanings in the New Testament, both derived from that original signification. It sometimes means to set two persons side by side, in the way of introducing and recommending the one to the other. It sometimes means to set two things side by side, in the way of confirming or proving the one by the other. It is used in the latter sense here. God not merely "commends," but "proves," His love by Christ's death. It is the one evidence which makes that often-doubted fact certain. Through it alone is it possible to hold the conviction that, in spite of all that seems to contradict the belief, God is Love. And so I wish to take the words in this sermon.

The Need for Proof That God Does Love

To hear some men speak, you would suppose that one of the simplest, clearest, and most indisputable of all convictions was the love of God. People are found in plenty who reject the distinctive teaching of Christianity because they say that the sterner aspects of the evangelical faith seem to them to limit, or to contradict, the great fundamental truth of all religion, as they take it, that God is Love. My friends, such people are kicking away the ladder by which they climbed. I venture to say that instead of the love of God being a plain, self-evident axiom, there needs very strong evidence to give it a secure lodging-place amongst our settled beliefs.

Do the world's religions bear out the contention that it is so easy and natural for a man to believe in a loving God? I think not. Comparative mythology has taught a great many lessons, and amongst others this, that, apart from the direct or indirect influences of Christianity, there is no creed to be found in which the belief in a God of love and in the love of God is unfalteringly proclaimed, to say nothing of being set as the very climax of the whole revelation. If this were the place, one could pass in review men's thoughts about God and ask you to look at all that assemblage of beings before whom mankind has bowed down. What would you find? Gods cruel, gods careless, gods capricious, gods lustful, gods mighty, gods mysterious, gods pitying—with a contempt mingled with the pity—their sorrows and follies of mankind. But in all the pantheons there is not a loving god.

Before Jesus Christ there was no such thought, or if it were there at all, it was there as a faint hope, a germ overlaid by other conceptions. Independent of Jesus Christ's influence, there is no such thought now. Where you find the death of Christ as the proof rejected and the conviction retained, as is often the case, you have only a sign that "the river of the water of life" has percolated to the roots of many a tree that grows far from its banks. It is Christ who has brought the fire of this conviction, in the broken reed of His dying flesh, and lodged it in the heart of humanity. So I say the love of God, as is proved by men's thoughts about Him, surely needs to be established on a basis of unmistakable evidence.

I add that all other evidences are insufficient. Do you appeal, in the fashion of Paley and the natural theologians, to the evidence of God in creation? Ah! you have invoked a very ambiguous oracle that seems to speak with two voices. I say nothing about the modification that that argument has necessarily assumed if the theory of evolution is accepted. I do not think it is destroyed, but it is profoundly modified. For if God put into matter the promise and the potency of all these variations, He must lie back of the process, and be conceived of as forecasting, if not guiding, the evolution which ends in development. So the argument has only changed in its form and is unaffected in its substance.

But, putting aside all that, you speak of the goodness of God around us. What about storms, earthquakes, disasters, contrivances of producing pain, the law of destruction by which the creatures live by the slaying of one another—what about all these things? "Nature, red in tooth and claw with rapine, shrieks against the creed," that God is Love. And if we have nothing but the evidence of nature, it seems to me that there are two voices speaking there: One says, "There is a good God;" the other says, "Either His power is limited, or His goodness is partial."

The same ambiguous issue comes from the evidence of human life. Ah! brethren, we have only to look into our own lives and to look round upon the awful sights that fill the world to make the robustest faith in the goodness and love of God stagger, unless it can stay itself against the upright stem of the cross of Christ.

Sentimentalists may talk, but the grim fact of human suffering, of wretched, hopeless lives, rises up to say that there is no evidence broad and deep and solid enough, outside of Christianity, to make it absolutely certain that God is Love.

There is another thing that makes necessary some irrefutable proof far firmer and stronger than any of these that I have been referring to. That is, that conscience rises up and protests, when it is awake, against such a notion, apart from the cross. Everybody who honestly takes stock of himself and conceives of God in any measure aright, must feel that sin has come in to disturb all the relations between God and man. And when once a man comes to say, "I feel that I am a sinful man, and that God is a righteous God; how can I expect that His love will distill in blessings upon my head?" there is only one answer—"Whilst we were yet sinners, Christ died for us."

So, for all these reasons I venture to lay it down as a principle, in spite of modern teaching of another sort, that the love of God is not a self-evident axiom, but needs to be proved.

The Death That Does Prove the Love

How do we know, in our own happy experiences, that love toward us exists in another heart? Surely, by act. Words are well (and words are acts, of a sort); but we want something more. Paul thinks that— mightier than all demonstrations of a verbal kind, in order to establish the fact of love in the Divine heart to men— there must be some conspicuous and unmistakable act that is the outcome of that love. So mark that, when he wants to enforce this great truth—the shining climax of all the gospel revelation of the love of God, he does not go back to Christ's gentle words, nor to His teaching of God as the Father. Paul does not point to anything that Christ says, but he points to one thing that He did, and he says, "There! that cross is the demonstration."

And, since it has a special bearing on my subject, I wish to emphasize that distinction and to beseech you to believe that you have not got within sight of the secret of Jesus, nor come near tapping the sources of His power if you confine yourselves to His words and His teaching, or even to the lower acts of His gentle life. You must go to the cross. It would have been much that Paul would have spoken with certitude and with sweetness else unparalleled of the love of God. But

words, however eloquent, however true, are not enough
for the soul to rest its weight upon. We must have
deeds, and these are all summed in "Christ died for
us."

Now, there are but two things that I wish to say
about this great proof of the love of God in act.

*First, Christ's death proves God's love, because Christ
is Divine.* How else do you account for that
extraordinary shifting of the persons in my text? "God
proves His love because Christ died?" How so? God
proved His love because Socrates died? God proved His
love because some self-sacrificing doctor went into a
hospital and died in curing others? God proved His
love because some man sprang into the sea and rescued
a drowning woman, at the cost of his own life? Would
such talk hold? Then I wish to know how it comes that
Paul ventures to say that God proved His love because
Jesus Christ died.

Unless we believe that Jesus Christ is the Eternal
Son of the Father, whom the Father sent, and who
willingly came for us men and for our redemption;
unless we believe that, as He Himself said, "He that
hath seen Me hath seen the Father" (John 14:9); unless
we believe that His death was the act, the consequence,
and the revelation of the love of God, who dwelt in
Him as in none other of the sons of men, I, for one,
venture to think that Paul is talking nonsense in my
text, and that his argument is not worth a straw. You
must come to the full-toned belief which, as I think,
permeates and binds together every page of the New
Testament—God so loved the world, and sent His Son
to be the propitiation for sins; that Son who in the
beginning was with God, and was God; and then a
flood of light is poured on the words of my text, and we
can adoringly bow the head and say, "Amen! God hath,
to my understanding, and to my heart, proved and
commended His love, in that Christ died for us!"

*The second thought about this death that proves the
love is, that it does so because it is a death for us.* That

"for us" implies two things: one, the voluntary act of God in Christ in giving Himself up to the death, the other the beneficial effect of that death. It was on our behalf. Therefore, it was the spontaneous outgush of an infinite love. It was for us in that it brought an infinite benefit. And so it was a token and a manifestation of the love of God such as nothing else could be.

Now, I wish to ask a question very earnestly: In what conceivable way can Christ's death be a real benefit to me? How can it do me any good? A sweet, a tender, an unexampled, beautiful story of innocence and meekness and martyrdom which will shine in the memory of the world, and on the pages of history, as long as the world shall last. It is all that; but what good does it do me? Where does the benefit to me individually come in? There is only one answer, and I urge you to ask yourselves if, in plain, sober, common sense, the death of Jesus Christ means anything at all to anybody, more than other martyrdoms and beautiful deaths, except upon one supposition, that He died for us, because He died instead of us. The two things are not necessarily identical, but, as I believe, and venture to press upon you, in this case they are identical. I do not know where you will find any justification for the rapturous language of the whole New Testament about the death of Christ and its benefits flowing to the whole world, unless you take the Master's own words, "The Son of Man came to minister, and to give His life a ransom instead of many" (Mark 10:45).

Ah, dear friends, there we touch the bedrock. That is the truth that flashes up the cross into luster before which the sun's light is but darkness. He who bore it died for the whole world and was the eternal Son of the Father. If we believe that, then we can understand how Paul here blends together the heart of God and the heart of Christ, and sets high above nature and her ambiguous oracles, high above providence and its many perplexities, and in face of all the shrinkings and fears of a reasonably alarmed conscience, the one truth, "God hath proved His love for us, in that while we were yet sinners, Christ died for us." Is that your faith, your notion of Christ's death and of its relation to the love of God?

The Love Which Is Proved by the Death

There is much bearing upon that in my text, which I can barely spare time to draw out. But let us think for a moment of the fact which is thus the demonstration of the love of God and try to realize what it is that that cross says to us as we gaze upon the silent Sufferer meekly hanging there. I know that my words must fall far beneath the theme, but I can only hope that you will listen to them charitably and try to better them for yourselves in your own thoughts.

I look, then, to the dying Christ, and I see there the revelation, because the consequence—of a love that is not called forth by any lovableness on the part of its objects. The apostle emphasizes the thought, if we render his words fully, because he says, "God proves His own love." It is a love which, like all that belongs to that timeless, self-determining Being, has its reason and its roots in Himself alone. We love because we discern the object to be lovable. God loves by what I may venture to call the very necessity of His nature. Like some artesian well that needs no pumps nor machinery to draw up the sparkling waters to flesh in the sunlight, there gushes up from the depths of His own heart the love that pours over every creature He has made. He loves because He is God.

In like manner, another word of my text bears upon this matter, for he says, "Whilst we were yet sinners, Christ died for us." Oh! brethren, it is only the gospel of a dying Christ that can calm the reasonable consciousness of discord and antagonism that springs in a man's heart when he lets his conscience speak. It is because He died for us that we are sure now that the black mountain-wall of our sin, which, to our own apprehension, rises separating between us and our God is, if I may so say, surged over by the rising flood of His love. The cross of Christ teaches me that, and so it is the gospel for men that know themselves to be sinners. Is there anything else that teaches it? I know not where it is, if there be.

That dying Christ, hanging there in the silence and the darkness of eclipse, speaks to me too, of a Divine love which, though not turned away by man's sin, is rigidly righteous.

I referred, at the beginning of my remarks, to the current, easy-going religion that says, "Oh! we do not want any of your evangelical contrivances for forgiveness. God is Love. That is enough for us." I venture to say that the thing which that form of thought calls love is not love at all, but pure weakness. Such in a king or in a father would be immoral. It is not otherwise in God. My brother! Unless you can find some means whereby the infinite love of God can get at and soothe the sinner's heart without periling God's righteousness, you have done nothing to the purpose. Such a one-eyed, lop-sided gospel will never work, has not worked, and it never will. But, when I think of my Christ bearing the sins of the world, I say to myself, "Herein is love. By His stripes we are healed," and in Him love and righteousness are both crowned and wondrously brought into harmonious oneness. Is there anything else that will do that? If there be, I, for one, know not what it is.

Again, when I look on the dying Christ I see a divine love, which is bounded by no limits of time or place. Look at that majestic and significant, *commendeth*, not *commended* or *proved*, as if it were a past fact, sliding away rapidly into the oblivion that wraps all past events as the world gets older, and its memory gets more burdened. It is "commendeth" today, as it commended eighteen hundred years ago.

Remember to whom Paul was speaking—people that had never seen Jesus Christ—many of whom had not been in the world when He left it. Yet He says "that cross stands there for you of this second generation as the present proof of eternal love."

And, my friends, it stands for us men and women in Manchester as truly as for the men and women of Galilee or of Rome. There is no limit of time at all, either to the power of the proof or to the love that it establishes. But today, as long ago of old, and as it will be in the remotest future, the cross of Christ towers up like some great mountain beacon, when all beneath is lost to sight, as the one eternal demonstration of an everlasting love.

And now, dear brethren, *proves* is a cold word. It is addressed to the head. *Commends* is a warmer word. It is addressed to the heart. It is not enough to establish the fact that God loves. Arguments may be wrought in frost as well as in fire; and if I have erred in any measure in that regard this evening, I ask pardon of Him and of you. But it is your hearts I want to get at— through your heads. I do not care to make you orthodox believers in a doctrine. That is all very well, but it is a very small part of our work. I want your hearts to be touched, and that Christ shall be not only the answer to your doubts, but the sovereign of your affections. Do you look on the death of Christ as a death for your sin? In the strength of the revelation that it makes the love of God, do you front the perplexities, the miseries of the world, and the raveled skeins of providence with calm, happy faces? And oh!—most important of all—do you meet that love with an answering love?

There are two passages of Scripture which contain the whole secret of a noble, blessed, human life. And here they are: "God so love the world, that He gave His only begotten Son, that whosoever believeth in Him shall not perish, but have everlasting life" (John 3:16). If that is your thought about God, you know enough about Him for time and eternity. "We love Him, because He first loved us" (1 John 4:19). If you can say that about yourself, all is well.

Dear friend, do you believe the one? Do you affirm the other?

The Atonement

George Campbell Morgan (1863-1945) was the son of a
British Baptist preacher and preached his first sermon
when he was 13 years old. He had no formal training
for the ministry, but his tireless devotion to the study
of the Bible helped him to become one of the leading
Bible teachers of his day. Rejected by the Methodists,
he was ordained into the Congregational ministry. He
was associated with Dwight L. Moody in the Northfield
Bible conferences and as an itinerant Bible teacher.
He is best known as the pastor of Westminster Chapel,
London (1904-17 and 1933-45). During his second term
there, he had Dr. D. Martyn Lloyd-Jones as his
associate.

He published more than 60 books and booklets, and
his sermons are found in *The Westminster Pulpit*
(London, Pickering and Inglis). This sermon is from
Volume 5.

George Campbell Morgan

7

THE ATONEMENT

You, being in time past alienated and enemies in your mind in your evil works, yet now hath He reconciled in the body of His flesh through death, to present you holy and without blemish and unreprovable before Him (Colossians 1:21, 22).

IN THIS COLOSSIAN letter are two brief declarations that may be said to embody its teaching. The first is that in which the apostle declares, "In Him," that is in the Lord Jesus Christ, "dwelleth all the fulness of the Godhead bodily" (2:9). The second is that in which he tells those Christians to whom he was writing, the saints at Colosse and the faithful in Christ Jesus, "in Him ye are made full." The theme of the letter is that of the glorious Christ, and of all the glories of the Christ at the disposal of His church in order that she may fulfill all the good pleasure of the will of God.

In the course of dealing with these great subjects, the apostle wrote some of the most wonderful things, if I may suggest such a distinction, that the New Testament contains concerning our Lord and Master. In Colossians 1 he deals with the threefold fact of Christ's glory; His glory in relation to His Father in that, He "is the image of the invisible God" (v. 15); His glory in relation to the whole creation in that, He is "the firstborn of all creation" (v. 15), all things coming by the word of His power, all things moving to the goal of His purpose, all things consisting, or being held together by Him; His glory in relation to the church, in that, He is the Head of the Church, "the firstborn from the dead" (v. 18); and, finally, He says of Him "that in all things He might have the preeminence" (v. 18).

It is not to be wondered at that in the midst of such spacious and wonderful declarations concerning the glory of Christ, the apostolic reference to the cross should be equally spacious and equally mysterious. It is in this whole great passage in which we see Christ in His relation to the whole cosmos, its Originator, its Sustainer, its Goal; that we also see Christ in His relation to the chaos, its Redeemer, its Reconciler, its Restorer. In this passage the apostle declares that through Christ the work of reconciliation is accomplished; not only between individual men and God, not only in the complex mystery of an individual life, not only in this world, but also in the heavens.

Thus the apostle places the cross of Christ at the very center of everything. As Christ Himself is at the center of all things, and as all things are upheld and made consistent by His power, so also at the center of all is His cross. The power of the cross is felt not only in the nearest things but also to the utmost bound of creation. The work of the cross must be ultimately measured, not merely by what it does within individual life, but by what it accomplishes in the heavens, among angels, and at last by what it has done in the being and nature of God, because by it righteousness and peace are able to meet together and to kiss each other.

In an atmosphere so full of glory, in the presence of declarations concerning our Lord and His cross so calculated to fill the soul with awe, we come to this central word, this word that touches us most nearly and most intimately, the word that reveals the way of our reconciliation.

This statement first reveals our need of reconciliation. Second, it declares the provision made by God in Christ and unveils the method thereof in so far as it can be unveiled for our eyes. Third, it makes clear to us the purpose of that reconciliation in the economy of God.

The need of reconciliation is made clear in the words, "You, being in time past alienated and enemies in your mind in your evil works." The way of reconciliation is declared in the words "reconciled in the body of His flesh through death." The ultimate purpose of reconciliation in the experience of man is declared in the last words, "to present you holy and without blemish and unreprovable before Him."

Our Need of Reconciliation

Let us at once interpret the meaning of *reconciliation* by the term *atonement*, always remembering the true and simple meaning of that word. Our fathers were accustomed to say that the word *atonement* means "at-one-ment." That has been contradicted, but it is a very interesting fact that the very last of our lexicographers, Murray, declares that to be the true meaning of the word. The verb *atone* is not that from which the substantive *atonement* is derived, for the substantive preceded the verb, and *at-one-ment* was a word used in our language before the verb *atone*. The word *atonement* does not actually reveal the method of reconciliation; rather, it describes the state of reconciliation. In our theological formulas we use the word to indicate the method that produces the result, and then we attempt to explain it. I am not using the word in that way now, but rather in the old and simplest sense, that of being brought into at-one-ment with God.

Is there a need for this? Has man lost his at-one-ment with God? The apostle declares that he has and describes his condition as, "alienated and enemies in your mind in your evil works." This is not mere rhetoric. It is a most careful setting forth of the truth concerning man in his sin, beginning with the profoundest, essential fact in human personality, the spiritual, which is alienated. In the next place it describes the mental attitude, the consciousness of human life, "enemies in your mind." And finally, it deals with that physical side of personality which is the expression of the spiritual, "in your evil works."

Alienated. The force of the word is not aliens. It is not the fact that they were aliens that was in the mind of the apostle, but the fact that they were alienated, and that suggests activity on the part of God. It presupposes a reason which it does not yet declare, but it declares an action, an action on the part of God. They were alienated, cut off from fellowship with God, and that by the act of God. Just as surely as reconciliation is in one of its profoundest aspects judicial, so also is the alienation that makes reconciliation necessary. Translate the Greek word literally and it reads, "you were made to be strangers," a common word at that time, used of those who had lost their citizenship.

I pause to lay all this stress upon the true meaning and value of this word because it involves a truth that we are in danger of forgetting. This word recognizes the sovereignty of God. We are very much inclined to speak today as though the fact that we are offspring of God puts us on some equality with God, which gives us warrant to talk to Him about our rights, to make terms with Him as to how He may deal with us, or even to descend low enough in the scale of blasphemy to declare what we would do if we were God. All this is the tendency of the hour.

In the presence of the cross, making the declaration of our need for reconciliation, the apostle declared that man is alienated from God by the act of God. That is perfectly righteous of God because of man's own sin— the sin of his own will, of his own choice—wherein he has turned away from God. The turning away from God on the part of man results in the definite act on the part of God by which He shuts man away from fellowship with Himself. "Your sins," said the prophet, "have separated between you and God" (Isaiah 59:2). That is the Old Testament declaration. It is exactly the same truth. Because of your sins, thundered the prophets to Israel of old, God has cut you off from fellowship.

The sinning man may still pray, may still continue to cross the threshold of the earthly house of God, may still take His name upon his lips, may still sing the songs of the sanctuary, may still intellectually attempt to apprehend the doctrines of Christianity; but he has no personal fellowship with God. God will not admit him to that fellowship. No man can see the Lord without holiness. No man can have fellowship with God while he is still in his sin.

Let us pass to the next phrase and phase. In the deepest fact of human life, men because of their sin are alienated from God, cut off from fellowship with him, spiritually dead in trespasses and sins. Therefore, they must be described in the words of the apostle as "Enemies in your mind." That is the consequence of alienation. Man's consciousness of God's attitude toward him in his sin creates the attitude of enmity toward God on the part of man. Let me state it this way. God is forever at war with human failure, making no terms with it, making no peace with it, making no excuse for it; therefore, man is forever at war with the will of God, which forbids his sin, which would interfere with his sin, which would take from him all the activities wherein he is destroying himself, and perpetuating evil in the universe of God. God is at war with sin in every man, and with every man who is sinning. God is angry with the wicked every day. The wrath of God abideth upon the ungodly. In the strange and mystic consciousness of every man, there is the conviction that this is the attitude of holiness toward his impurity, of righteousness toward his wrong, of purity toward his corruption; and he answers it with the attitude of rebellion, and of persistent enmity. Man hates God because God hates man's sin.

This is illustrated by the attitudes of men toward God in the world today. I am not speaking merely of blatant and brutal attacks upon the Christian religion. I am thinking also of the objection there is among men everywhere to the mention of the name of God, as though God had some cruel purpose toward man. We may talk of politics, of play, of books, but if we talk about God, we are considered objectionable. Why is it that men will not talk about God? Because they are enemies in their mind against God. Why? Because they know that God is at war with sin, that God excludes the willfully sinning from fellowship, and will make no terms with their sin. Therefore, men are at enmity against God.

What is the final result? It is expressed in the words, "In your evil works." All the activities of life are evil, when they are activities out of harmony with the will of God. We look upon these activities and divide between them as between vulgar and respectable, but all life that is godless life is evil life. The man who is alienated from God and has no direct, immediate contact with Him and fellowship with Him—no conscious fellowship with God—that man is at enmity against God. If he does not blaspheme His name, if he does not write a book to prove He does not exist, nevertheless, he objects to hearing of Him with the result that the physical life is a life of evil, "in your evil works."

Thus, while an initial act of sin called for alienation, continuance in sin results from alienation; and therein is revealed the utter helplessness of man in his sin. The profoundest fact in human life is the spiritual, and if it is excluded from God, alienated from God, then that spirit life has no right of entry within the veil. It has not ceased to be, but it has no way of appropriating the resources which strengthen it. It is offspring of God, yet excluded from fellowship with God. Therefore, the mind is at enmity against God, and the works are evil works.

The Way of Reconciliation

How can there be reconciliation between God and a man in that state? We turn immediately to the next words of our text; words full of sublimity, to be considered with great reverence, "Now hath He reconciled in the body of His flesh through death." In the words, "in the body of His flesh," the apostle refers to the actual human life of Jesus of Nazareth. Behold it for a moment, and think of it, as it stands in vivid, startling, almost appalling contrast to the picture of humanity which we have been considering.

Man is alienated from God. This Man lived the life

of perfect fellowship with God. Man, because of alienation in spirit from God and the consequent enmity of mind against God, is in his bodily life performing evil works. This Man, because of His friendship with God, went about doing good, good works instead of evil works. This Man is of my humanity; but by this contrast He is seen to be entirely different from that which I am.

We know the meaning of Paul's words, "alienated," "enemies in your mind," "in evil works." We know every phase of the description experimentally. We know their inter-relation; that because we were away from God, our minds were at enmity against God, and the works of our lives were works of evil. Knowing these things, we come into the presence of this Man in the body of His flesh. Everything is of our nature, but is not of the nature of our living. We were alienated! He lived in perfect fellowship! Our mind was enmity! He was the Friend of God, the One in whom alone that phrase has ever been perfectly fulfilled and manifested in meaning to the sons of men. Our works were evil. He did only good works.

Now, let us understand this. We have not yet reached the realm of reconciliation. Not by what He was in the body of His flesh can He reconcile me to God. The whole stupendous truth is declared in the next two words, "through death."

The incarnation is not reconciliation. In its very nature it cannot be, for God in Christ, in the perfection of the life of Jesus, is the sternest foe of sinning man. That fair and beautiful life condemns my faulty and sinning life.

The teaching that fell from His lips—the ethic He revealed as being the will of God for man—simply brings me to a consciousness of my humiliation. It is impossible for me to realize that high ideal.

All His deeds were deeds directed against the evil works in which I live. If I have nothing in Jesus other than that unveiling of divine purpose, and that picture of a Man who is of my nature but lived in other relationships, then there is still no reconciliation. I am still at war with God in Him. If Jesus Christ were merely a Teacher, a Social Reformer, He could win this country and all civilized countries within six months. But it is because He still stands for heart purity, for rectitude of spirit with God, for the fundamental things of holiness and righteousness and truth, that men are against Him. Not in the body of His flesh—with its revelation of the true meaning of every human life and the divine intention for human life—is there reconciliation, nor can there be.

This Man died. Now, if our reconciliation could have been by incarnation, then that death was the most awful reflection on the power and wisdom of God that has occurred in all human history. Unless there be some profound meaning; unless it be, as Peter said it was, of "the determinate counsel and foreknowledge of God" (Acts 2:23), unless there be something infinitely more than the capture of a victim of brutal humanity and his murder, then the permission of that murder undermines my faith in the goodness of God and in His righteousness, for the problem of evil is focused here. Sigh as you will over the sorrows and sighings of humanity over the problem of evil—there is no problem of evil in London—slum or suburb—in China, in Africa, or in India, comparable to that of the cross. What is the meaning of that death, the death of One who in the body of His flesh lived a life of perfect harmony with God, realizing the divine purpose, illumining the divine meaning, and satisfying the divine requirements?

"You . . . hath He reconciled in the body of His flesh through death." This declaration does not attempt to tell all the secrets. The New Testament never has made that attempt, and those men who have made the attempt have proved their inability.

"Through death." If we would interpret the meaning of the word *death* there, we must do so by remembering the Person referred to. The image of the invisible God; the firstborn of all creation; the Origin and Sustainer and Goal of the cosmos; in a mystery entirely baffling my poor finite mind, He came into flesh, and He died. That is the one death. There is no other death by the side of that. The death is infinite because the Person is infinite. In the body of His flesh "through death." Here is the manifestation, the unveiling. Just as in His life, the grace and glory of the Father are unveiled by their veiling in the flesh; so in His death, of infinite passion and pain, is an unveiling. We must interpret the death by the One who died. There is no analysis of this, no plumbing of its depths, no possibility of satisfactory theorizing!

"Through death." What is death? Death is the penalty of sin. We cannot escape that word *penalty*. Death is the penalty of sin, not merely its issue, its outcome; that also for the method of God's penalty is always poetic. Penalty is the fruitage of sin necessarily. Then here is the mystery, that the Sinless died.

May God help us to remember this: Before that cross of Calvary we never can see everything. These are some of the things we may see. In the mystery of that cross, this One upon whom our eyes have been resting is not in conflict with God. He is working together with God. "God was in Christ reconciling the world unto Himself" (2 Corinthians 5:19); not merely in the days of public teaching, not merely in the days of miracle and wonder-working, not merely in the subsequent days of resurrection light, but surely also in the cross, "God was in Christ reconciling." "You...now hath He reconciled in the body of His flesh through death."

That act of death no man can fathom. It excludes me forevermore as I try to understand its deepest meaning. So far as I am allowed to say this, let me say it: I have never read a book on the atonement that has quite satisfied me, but every one has given me some new and true view of it. Still, I have never read a book that has satisfied me. There are quantities and elements that defy analysis and elude comprehension. That death, at the heart of the universe, is felt to its remotest bound, for He reconciles all things in the earth and in the heavens to Himself, and in that great reconciliation, great because of the Person and the death, I find my possibility for the man who is alienated, that he may come into fellowship with God; for the man who is at enmity against God; for the man whose works are evil, that he may come to fruitfulness in all good works before God.

Now, I am certainly touching things we are all familiar with, for I am touching the realm of the experience of the saints. There are men and women, thank God, many of them in this house who know I am speaking the language of their own experience, men and women who can say, "Our fellowship is with the Father and with His Son Jesus Christ," by which they mean God speaks to them and they speak to Him. They call to God and He hears them. Men may indulge in all the speculative arguments against prayer that they please, but they will never disturb the certain confidence of these people. They know, they hear the voice amid the roar of the city, they hear the voice in the silence of their own heart. God speaks to us, we speak to God. We are no longer alienated, made to be strangers; we are made fellow-citizens with the saints, and fellow-citizenship with the saints means right of access to God.

We know that God is, not because you have argued for Him, or demonstrated Him by syllogism, but because He speaks and we hear, we speak and He answers. That possibility was created through this death. It is by what that death has done for us in our own moral consciousness that we have found our way to God. It is out of that consciousness of sin forgiven, which in this same chapter the apostle speaks of as "our redemption the forgiveness of sins" (v. 14), that we have come to fellowship with Him. That fellowship means friendship, we love to speak of Him and all His wondrous ways. In the days of formalism, when Malachi delivered His message, he declared, "Then they that feared the Lord spake one with another and the Lord hearkened and heard" (3:16). God is still hearkening and hearing men and women who love Him, as they speak of His name out of friendship with Him, and love of Him.

This fellowship and friendship issues in the possibility of fruitfulness in goodness. Very slowly does the full fruit come! We know that all too well; but thank God, He is patient with us. It is first the blade, then the ear, then the full corn in the ear, and He with patience waits for the final fruitage.

The Purpose of Reconciliation

The ultimate purpose is that we should be holy. That is, we are no longer alienated but in fellowship with life, holy in character as He is. We should be without blemish, that is, no longer enemies, but by love satisfying love. And we should be unreprovable, that is, no longer evil workers, but pleasing Him in all things.

Let this last matter be most carefully observed. The work of reconciliation which He did is necessary to a reconciled life. Concerning this there is very much false thinking today. The atonement is too often spoken of as though it afforded a mere provision of pardon. It does that; but infinitely more. Its results are judicial, necessary to experience. It is judicial, but it is radical; it touches character.

Atonement was necessary. Until alienation and enmity and evil works are dealt with, there can be no reconciliation. God cannot be reconciled to man in his sin. Man must be reconciled to God in His holiness. The possibility of holiness is the true gospel hope for those who know their alienation, and who in response to the constraint of the Holy Spirit enter into fellowship by the way of the cross. We may find our way back into intimate personal fellowship with God because

> Nothing in my hand I bring
> Simply to Thy cross I cling.

If we so come, we shall know the reconciliation. It will be reconciliation that begins with the consciousness of God, issues in love of God, and finds its crown in the works that are pleasing to God.

What Brought Christ to the Cross?

Arthur John Gossip (1873-1954) preached this sermon shortly after the sudden death of his beloved wife. He ministered in Great Britain as the pastor of four different churches, as an army chaplain, and as a professor of practical theology at Trinity College, Glasgow, Scotland.

This sermon comes from his book *The Galilean Accent*, published in Edinburgh in 1926 by T. & T. Clark.

Arthur John Gossip

8

WHAT BROUGHT CHRIST TO THE CROSS?

Had they known it, they would not have crucified the Lord of Glory (1 Corinthians 2:8).

WHATEVER ELSE IS to be made of it, everyone feels that the cross stands out a hideous tragedy, a dreadful fact black as a splash of ink upon our human records. "They have crucified the Lord of Glory!" gasps Paul in horror. And as often as it comes in sight of Calvary, the heart of mankind echoes that shuddering cry, stands rooted to the spot, staring incredulously at what can't be true; yet there it really is!

How did it happen, this appalling thing? What sudden orgy of insanity overwhelmed for one mad day the kindly human nature that we know so well, and swept it headlong into this? For we feel hotly that it must have been something monstrous, inexplicable, blown in from the darkness round us, that was guilty of that horror. Yet the last haunting terror of it is that it was brought about by ordinary mortals like ourselves, kindly and likable in many ways, no doubt—their children ran with happy shouts to father that day he came home from Calvary, well satisfied, as he kept telling his wife as he played with his little one, with the day's admirable work—that it was not something unthinkable and gross and obviously devilish that was responsible to our Lord's cross; but that it was set up by the quite ordinary, decent and respectable little sins of decent and respectable people, by the kind of thing into which we are all apt to drift every other day. Let us remember that with a great shivering awe, lest in our lives too there rings out that sound of hammering, as the nails run home.

"The past throws light on the future," says Guicciardini, "because the world was ever on the same make; and all that is or will be in another day has already been, and the same things return, only with different names and colors. It is not everyone who knows them under the new face, but the wise know them." And age by age the Lord Christ is crucified. And we too have crowded eagerly to Calvary and nailed Him to His cross, and laughed up into His face, and watched Him die, and gone our way well pleased and much relieved that we have hustled Him out of the way—yes, even we.

The Role of the Pharisees

Who brought this infamy about, who did it? Well, to begin with then, there were the Pharisees. As a class they disliked Christ, and they said so frankly. They resented the intrusion of this layman—and an ill-educated man at that, they snarled—into their own domain. His teaching, or much of it, seemed to them sheer blasphemy. His habits they thought just disgusting. You can always tell a man by the kind of company he keeps, they sneered, and, with a meaning shrug of the shoulders, glanced scornfully at the sorry rabble of impossible persons with whom Christ was not ashamed to mingle. Yet they were zealously religious people, keen church-going folk as we would say, more keen and zealous by far than we are. They prayed, they fasted, they disciplined themselves with a thoroughness along their own lines that might well make us with our cheap amateur haphazard methods much ashamed. They were good people in their way, devout and desperately in earnest so far as they saw.

But they made two mistakes. They were apt, as Jesus told them bluntly, to keep their life and their religion in separate compartments, and to try to compound for the one by offering that other. To pray and fast and keep their multitudinous rules was hard enough, but after all, that was a good deal easier than to be kind and unselfish when that clashed with their desires. They hoped and felt that it might do instead. They prayed long and ardently, but it had small effect upon their characters. Their temper, prayers or no prayers, remained still uncurbed, the fierceness of their animosities and party spirit were hardly checked. Nor did that seem to vex them, or to make them feel that something was wrong somewhere. That that was the end of religion had not somehow struck them. And so, while praying hard, and thronging to the Temple day by day, they planned Calvary, and worked it out triumphantly into a fact of history.

This is a very solemn warning for us all. For Jesus tells us very gravely that His experience of men has taught Him that this, or something like this, is a very common failing. People can be eagerly, even fussily religious, and yet nothing may come of it in their characters. And He keeps begging each of us to make quite certain that it is not so in his case. He pursues us in this matter with blunt, awkward, pertinacious questions, difficult to face. These prayers of yours, He asks, what are they doing in you? Do they end with themselves? Are they really making you more like God; or do you run them up as a cheap substitute for worthy living? Your knowledge of the Father, and of the brotherhood of man, is the one forcing you to live your life too in God's way? Is the other making your conscience more acute to things about you which formerly you didn't notice, so that you can't pass by now upon the other side, happy in your own comforts, until these wrongs are righted?

The thrills in a service when our souls are moved may become only a kind of luxury, and even an intemperance; and it has no religious value unless that emotion ends in definite action. "I fell in," says Bunyan, "with the customs of the time, to wit, to go to church twice a day, and there would I sing and pray with the foremost, yet retaining my evil life." What if we, too, are like that merchant whose bales, won at the price of such far traveling and sacrifice, on being opened, fell into mere dust? Hot, perspiring, diligent, that man, says Christ, is simply losing all his labor and creating bitter disappointment and sheer ruin for himself. He is building upon sand, and the first gush of temper, the first claim of selfishness, the first evil day, will sweep away all his so-called religion. They are mere planks and wreckage tossing for a second on wild waters, and then gone.

But, though it seems much the less of the two, it was their other error that proved far the more tragic. These Pharisees had minds that were old-fashioned, narrow, bigoted. They stood for the old ways and the accepted forms of things. They themselves would have said that they were men of principle, and not to be cajoled aside. But in reality they were simply inhospitable to new light, frankly incredulous that there was any more to find. To them change meant, of necessity, degeneracy. Their particular form of stating truth was final. To their fathers there had been vouchsafed amazing spiritual experiences; and they, the children, not only remembered them with gratitude and founded on them, as was right and fitting, but took it for granted that the way in which God acted then must be the way in which He would act now, if He did so at all. They forgot, indeed, that God was alive in their day too, that even the best in history did not exhaust Him, that there was "still much light to break forth from His word." To them the book was closed, the revelation and their understanding of it were alike, they felt, completed. They had no hope of progress—no expectation of any further news bursting in to them from God. When rumors of that reached them, at once and without examination, they discredited them as impossible and, on the face of things, quite evidently unauthentic. For, in effect, boldly they laid it down that their poor passing conceptions were a perfect reflection of God's thoughts. Their theories were not simply theories but the eternal facts, which could not be improved, and which must not be altered. Moses said this! Moses did that! they said; and for them that was final. And when Jesus stood forth and said, No doubt he did; but I now tell you something wholly different and vastly better, they clapped quick horrified hands over their outraged ears and would not listen. They resolved at once that this appalling person must be hustled out of the way. For if these notions of His spread abroad, why, plainly, there is an end of religion! And it was that that set up the cross on Calvary!

That thoughtful but forgotten author, Arthur Helps, remarks with truth that, "To be tolerant of intolerant people, to see how natural their intolerance is, and, in fact, thoroughly to comprehend it and feel it, is the last stage of tolerance, which few men, I suppose, in the world attain." Faced by that drastic test, once again Christ stands forth supreme. It was with compassion that He looked at these dull, angry souls shut into their cramped corner of a world, mistaking their dim, smoky rushlights for God's sun. The prophets grow quite fierce over that habit of the human mind, either to look back wistfully to the great days of long ago when God really was God, and things really happened, whereas now our lot is cast in a flat and prosaic time, or else to assume that what they have is all that they can have. Don't keep talking of Egypt, they fairly shout, almost shaking them. For if you, too, have only a touch of the faith they had then, now in our day things far more wonderful will happen in your own experience! Don't rest content with such glimpses of truth as you have caught. Look here, and here, and here, at all the glories in it hidden from you still. And they are hot and angry.

But Christ, remembering how natural it is, is very gentle. No one, He says, prefers new wine to old; and to be satisfied with the accustomed, the familiar, that in which one was brought up, is all but universal. He did not think it strange that many did not take to Him at once, and He was content to wait for their slow stumbling minds. Nonetheless, again and again He urges on us to keep our minds open and our hearts expectant—on the outlook for God. Not to do so, He indicates, is a moral failure that may have tragic consequences. And with fearsome reason! For when you come to look at things, it was no hideous and ugly sin, but just a prejudice, a narrowness of mind, a lack of mental hospitality, just an unwillingness to credit or even consider what was new and unaccustomed, just a dislike of being jostled out of one's settled lines of thought, just that, that set up Christ's cross upon Calvary!

When today one hears some people, passionate in their dislike of any innovation in theology or in religious thinking, proudly declaring it is loyalty to Christ that makes them take their stand, the fact stares at us that it was such people, animated in their day by just such motives—quite sure that they too were right and working for God's honor—who crucified our Lord. Its every age since then, they have continued doing it. It was when Mansoul fell that old crabbed Mr. Prejudice, with sixty deaf men under him, was set to guard Eargate. And it was that sinister guard that was the crucifixion squad that day Christ died, their hands that pushed Him forward, that laid Him on the cross, that ran the spear into His side—"old, angry, ill-conditioned Prejudice"—and his deaf ears and his inhospitable heart.

Are our hands clean? It is so easy to lose the gallant spirit of adventure that follows truth unflinchingly wherever truth may lead, to settle down and go no farther, to imagine that our poor little bundle contains everything that is of value, and to refuse to undo it again to pack in the new finds, to grow tired of always realizing that our thoughts of Christ are utterly inadequate, and so once more the walls, beginning to rise, have to come down and we must start rebuilding on a wider plan.

"God offers to every mind its choice between Truth and Repose," said Emerson. "Take which you please. You can never have both." We choose repose and let truth go. And yet in the New Testament, however high they pitched their thoughts of Christ, they found these couldn't anything like meet the facts that came crowding in upon them from their own experience, that they must make their thinking of Him vastly ampler still, and they kept doing it joyously. And, indeed, it is a poor tribute to Christ to say that we have come to the end of Him and know everything in Him there is to know; that the men of Nicea or Westminster, or even Paul, saw out to the end of the universe, and that there are no other stars, no further constellations to be found and charted. Always then we cease growing, we have started to decay. When water is not running, it is getting sour and stale and just a trifle smelly.

> Thought's a strange land—
> Some dig its fields with diligence,
> Some pass through it steadfastly, like pilgrims to the
>   Sepulchre,
> Some haste in dust and heat—toward what goal?
> Some climb its difficult hills, and clouds receive them
>   from our sight,
> Some take a neat villa, and plant geraniums in their
>   borders,
> And test the drains, and trim the wandering roses,
> And set up a paling to hide the restless road,

says Miss Underhill. Most of us do that last. For we are tired of footing it. We hide the restless road and settle down in some snug corner that we think will do. But she, for one, is all for pushing on and on, until the marshes and the salt winds and the strange voyaging birds make clear that we are near the sea.

> There on the fringes of thought when night is falling,
> I'll wait the invading tide.

Give Christ a mind like that and He will lead you ever deeper. Yes, but do we give it to Him? Are you never afraid that had you lived in His day you also, to a certainty, would have been hot against Him? Suppose it had been in our time a young man suddenly emerged out of an obscure Highland village, a tradesman in a little country way, who had never been much out of His own valley, and, talking in that provincial accent of His, told us that our accredited teachers were in many ways all wrong and our religion largely obsolete, that He had come to show us a more excellent way, a far truer faith, would we listen to Him any more than they did then? Do we listen when He does send His messengers to us with some new light? "Christ," said Tertullian, "did not call Himself the custom, but the truth." And while we are all loyal worshipers of custom, truth has few real disciples. Always it has had to fight its way to victory through hostile minds, distrustful and suspicious. Are you never afraid, I say, that at the last He may answer and say, In what way are you different from My murderers long ago? I am the Truth; and you, too, have denied Me entrance, would have none of Me, tried, as they did, to throttle Me! It was not something monstrous, it was sins like yours that long ago did Me to death. Aye, and yours, too, have often hindered Me.

"I observe," wrote Jonathan Edwards in his Diary, "that old men seldom have any advantage of new discoveries, because these discoveries are beside a way of thinking they have long been used to. Resolved, therefore, that if ever I live to years I will be impartial to hear the reason of all pretended discoveries, and receive them, if rational, how long soever I have been used to another way of thinking." Such an entry in the diary of Caiaphas or Annas, lived out, would have saved us the cross. Glancing up awe-struck at what sins like ours can do, let us, too, pledge ourselves to that, praying God for the open mind that recognizes Jesus when He comes.

The Role of the Saducees

And then there were the Sadducees. They held all the high places in the church, yet they had lost all spirituality, and indeed all belief in it. Religion was all very well, they said, but really, to get things done, you must look, not in that direction, but to politics. The axioms on which pious people founded were all more than doubtful, utterly unprovable, and almost certainly untrue. There was no resurrection—that, at least, was certain—no rewards and punishments hereafter; this brief life of ours was really all. A soul? Oh yes, no doubt there was a soul. But what was wanted was not brooding over that. Give us plain, practical measures of reform for this life here, and, not a doubt of it, the soul will take care of itself. And this upsetting person was becoming troublesome with His insistence upon secondary things—or so they conceived them—and was breeding trouble where they wanted peace and quiet. Yes, they felt, He were better away; and in the Council they, too, voted death.

And isn't all that very typical of our own day? If you wanted a label for us, would you find a better one than a Sadducean age? We also are not worrying about immortality, hardly believe in it, or at least are not sure. We, too, have limited ourselves to this dust-speck of time, leaving unclaimed the vast inheritance beyond of which Christ told us. We, too, are putting all our zeal and passion and enthusiasm into things of this earth here, ay, and material things at that, quite certain that that is the only road to progress, and that this everlasting chatter about the soul is quite beside the point.

They are all so earnest, and so certain, work so hard, are animated often by such lofty motives, are so sure that there is really no manner of need for Christ. Given this, and this, and this, each of them pushing forward his particular panacea, the world will manage very well. To talk about Christ and changing people's hearts and making us new creatures is merely to lose precious time and wander from the practical into vague daydreaming of which nothing comes. And year by year their voices grow a little harder, and they eye Christ more and more askance, feel sourly that He is a bit of a nuisance and a stumbling block to progress, keeping people quiet who should not be quiet, lulling them with these dim immaterial, fantastic, spiritual hopes of His which they think have no body, and can't save. Once more the whisper grows, "Were He not far better away?" Meantime we can ignore Him, they say; and they do. How many do!

Today, too, there is a great shouting for Barabbas, for the man of action: we, too, believe in politics and economics, but religion? Oh! no doubt there is a soul! But, set their circumstances right, and men will need no Savior, will soon show that they can take care of themselves! If, said Christ once, if the light that is in thee be darkness, how great is that darkness! If the enthusiasms and nobilities of an age, the cures and remedies for which it works with such eager self-sacrifice, are shallow, superficial, touching none of the real roots of the disease, what then? And still Christ holds to it, as He did in His own day full as ours is now of social sores and of tremendous economic problems, that in the last resort nothing can save the world but a new race of men and women, with new aims and ends and likings, and a new unselfishness and ardor of self-sacrifice. And still that angers men, and they rise up and cast Him out. We are all members of the council before which He is tried. And how does your heart vote? This is a Sadducean age, and in the mass we think with them entirely.

The Role of Judas

And there was Judas, that unhappy soul. Always in thinking of him we must start from this, that Christ loved Judas, Christ believed in Judas, Christ chose Judas with long prayer and deliberation as one of the twelve men whom He loved best to have beside Him, and of whom He hoped the most. Judas was a great soul, or had the makings of that in him. And when we come upon that horror, scarcely human, lying mangled there at the cliff foot, instinctively we look up, and with a shudder of fear and pity see how high he once walked in glory, and from what he fell to this.

The gospel writers are frankly not fair to their fallen colleague. Always that ghastly end of his there before their eyes, and from the very first they find it difficult to mention him without adding with that shiver of soul, they, who could tell the story of the crucifixion without one hot word concerning anyone, "who also betrayed Him."

Yet, far from deepening the tragedy, they rather lessen it by that; because, so doing, unconsciously they leave the impression on the reader's mind that almost he was chosen for the traitor's part, as an actor is cast to be the villain of the piece, and is marked villain from the start. But it was far more terrible than that. As you will never understand Macbeth until you take it in that it is a most noble nature we are watching crumbling there to ruin, so is it here. How did it happen, and Christ's confident dreams and hopes for him go out in such a starless night?

Some say that Judas saw the game was lost, and in a kind of maddened fury sought revenge on the man who had fooled him, robbing him of long years of his life. Some, not the least De Quincey, seeing, surely, deeper, say that Judas' sin was rather this—that Christ's prolonged delay amazed him—set his mind arguing. Is there not here a lack of nerve? Does He not see the tide is at the full, and He must launch out now? That it is turning; that if anything is ever to be done, then it must be at once; that it is running out faster and faster? And still Christ let chance after chance, as Judas judged, go by, and waited, and for what? Things were not growing better, but much worse. The opposition of the leaders had been given time to harden and lay plans. The people had lost much of that first eager passion of reckless enthusiasm with which, had it been seized at once, and rightly used, anything long ago might have been done. Christ was drifting, Judas felt, straight on the rocks. But vigorous action even yet might save the situation; and he planned to bring Christ to a test that He could not evade, to place Him in such a position as would lay compulsion on Him to take action, force his hand, make Him strike. He had lost patience with Christ, thought His plans were maladroit and crude and clumsy and by far too slow. Judas was looking for a short cut; he thought that he had found it; he took it—and it ended in that horror and the cross!

Too ingenious! Perhaps. Who can see clearly in that utter blackness, or say, with conviction, of a thing so ghastly, thus and thus it must have been?

And yet if that really was Judas' sin, if in a kind of blundering way he meant well, thinking that he knew better than his Master and because he could not wait for Him and His slow, sure, unhurried ways, sought cleverly to force His hand, God pity us! For are we not all apt to do just that! Is the church ever quite free from a half-bewildered, half-fretful impatience with Him, that can't trust to the steady drip, drip of the weekly services soaking into men's souls, that is irritated by the seeming resultlessness of His appointed methods, must have the kingdom break in with a rush and a loud noise and all men having to take note of it, keeps seeking for a swift immediate revival, not at God's time but now in ours, devising desperate expedients, trying to whistle up the winds of God! And they won't come. And these futilities we thought so wise and good and clever end in nothing except robbing people of their hopes, and so delaying what was in God's mind to give us, what was coming, and might have been here by now, had we not rushed in with our fatuous nothings, our machine-made revivals, our grotesque improvings upon Christ.

It is not so that real revivals rise, but, says Christ, like the winds. We hear the sound thereof, but cannot tell whence they have come, or where they go. A miner coming home from work is greeted in a courteous fashion by a friendly stranger, and somehow there on the road there rises up within his heart a passion of affection for his fellowmen which makes him give his life for them, and sweeps them by the thousand into the kingdom! "By Thine agony and bloody sweat, by Thy cross and passion, good Lord deliver us," a parson drones on in a cold age in a cold church at a cold service, with a few drowsy people scattered thinly, here and there, only half listening, if that. And suddenly the meaning of the words, breaking through long familiarity, rushes at one woman, seizes on her imagination, makes her see the thing and realize that this is not mere words but a shuddering fact; and a sob bursts from her, and that emotion spreads all through the church, and out and over a wide stretch of land, and changes lives unnumbered everywhere it passes.

God works in His own time, in His own ways. And if we try to dictate to Him, to demand it must be now, and in this fashion we have planned, only confusion comes of that. If we would cease our cunning engineering, our hot organizing, our continual talking and conferring, of which nothing ever seems to come but more conferring, if we would sit quiet and reverent in God's presence, and worship Him, and wait, and give His voice a chance of reaching men instead of ours, how much more might we see! For does our fussiness and cleverness do anything except this? Like Judas, we get in Christ's way and hinder Him, we who had meant to help, were so sure we could help, and had found the very way to do it! It was impatience with His methods, it was thinking he knew better than his Master, it was running on ahead of Him, that, think some, was the sin of Judas and that brought Christ to His cross. And who of us is not guilty of that?

The Role of Pilate

And Pilate, surely as pathetic a figure as there is in human history. A Roman, with a Roman's sense of justice, he knew at once that these charges against Christ were faked. With a curt question or two, he had the poor, bribed, muddled witnesses tripping and falling over their own impossible story, or contradicting one another at all points, quite evidently twisting innocent words into sinister meanings which they did not carry in the Accused's mouth. Tools, thought the man upon the judgment seat, and looked contemptuously at the hot faces showing through the doors, shouting and bawling yonder, half beside themselves with rage, though they would come no further into a Gentile court, these holy men upon this holy day, lest they might be polluted! How he despised and hated them! The man was hesitant to refuse them, being quite clear that there was really nothing against the strange silent Prisoner, so he tried hard to get Him off. And yet he signed the order for the crucifixion, and goes down in history, hooted and pelted with the infamy of every race. Why did he not leap to his feet and cry, "This is mere malice and not a substantial charge. The Prisoner is acquitted! And as for you, be off with you, lest you stand in His place!" Why, like a noble creature caught fast in a trap, does he only snarl and show his teeth, and struggle and long to hurl himself at his taunting enemies, and yet cannot break free?

They say it was old sins that troubled him, the past failures of the man that made things difficult for him now. There had been days when he had been too hectoring and domineering; so at least these impossible people said, though he himself denied it still. At all events, protesting to Rome, they had won the Emperor's ear, and humble their governor. And that must not happen again. Ah me! is not this life of ours a fearsome thing? Take care! take care! For if you sin that sin, be sure that somehow you will pay for it. And it may be at how hideous a price! So Pilate found in his day; so you, too, will find in ours.

> Our acts follow us from afar,
> And what we have been makes us what we are.

Only God knows what may come out of that, if you give way to it. Pilate was curt and domineering to the Jews one day. And it was because of that that months later his unwilling hands set up the cross of Christ; unwilling—but they did it. Take you care! For sin is very merciless. If you have had the sweet, it will see to it that you quaff the bitter to the very dregs. Think, think, and take you care!

Yes, but there is another very terrible fact. Fitz-James Stephen thought that Pilate's report of Christ's trial would make, could it be found, one of the most arresting state papers in history. And this is not only because of the Prisoner's personality, but because of the strong case that Pilate could make out for himself. There had been trouble before; there was always trouble with these pestilent Jews, with their mad hearts and touchy patriotism, quick to read offense in just nothing at all, and so unyielding about even their smallest rights. And Rome had laid it down that they must not be irritated. And yet here out of nowhere the old trouble was breaking out once more, and that at the worst possible time in the whole year, when the city was thronged and overflowing far into the country upon every side with multitudes of fanatical creatures, two million of them, it is said, only too ready and willing to be inflamed. These wretched priests would soon have this inflammable mass ablaze, and once more the gutters would be running blood. And that was not to be. The orders given him were strict that bloodshed was to be avoided, and that peace must be kept unbroken. And thus, looking at it from Pilate's standpoint, it comes down to this that it was to keep peace Christ's cross was set up on Calvary.

"It is expedient that one man die for the people," so Caiaphas announced. And Pilate, put in a cruel dilemma, came at last to that of it too. The Man was innocent. But did he set Him free—far worse was bound to happen; lives by the score would be sacrificed; and who could say where it would end? We must have peace. That was the one fixed point. And yet he hesitated, was unwilling. If only this had happened any other time! But with these Passover crowds about I cannot risk it. Peace we must have; and He must die. Quite plainly Pilate was impressed by Christ. Yet no doubt there is something in what Luther says. "Pilate took our Savior Christ to be a simple, honest, ignorant man, one perchance come out of a wilderness; a simple fellow, a hermit who knew or understood nothing of the world or of government." Yes, it was a pity, but He must die.

For us, looking on, it is easy to say that if the Man was innocent then let the heavens fall, but let justice be done. Yet not so long ago, in our own empire, a mob gathered where they had been forbidden, and a volley was fired, several volleys; and a thrill of horror swept us. But when those in authority stated that in their belief not to have fired meant an uprising and ugly massacres over a widespread area, we all settled down again, reflecting that it was a dreadful position in which they were placed, and no doubt they did what was best where nothing could be really good; and said no more about it. they must judge, they there upon the spot. Pilate, too, had to judge upon the spot. And, looking long at Jesus, slowly he brought himself to vote for peace.

And we had better think of that. For today we are all agog for peace—must have it. For us, too, that seems to be our one fixed point. And it is little wonder. For those who have once seen war have no desire ever again to see it. The thing is an insanity. For, quite obviously, to hurl chunks of metal at each other can prove nothing as to the original dispute. And we do well to labor zealously to make it a bad dream, and a forgotten horror left behind. For no man can imagine what another war with all the devilments of science thrown in to the full would be.

Yet we can go too far in our pursuit of peace. Is our zeal for it altogether pure, or partly that of a tired world that is not going to make any further sacrifices? Peace! Peace! we cry. Yet, after all, is peace the main thing? What about righteousness? Was Pilate right? And are we not beginning to slip down into his mood. Two little nations begin snarling at each other. And we are very bold. Be off, we say; and they slink away, making faces at each other. But a great power bullies a little one, and hotly announces it will brook no interference, that this touches its national honor. And we all carefully gaze the other way. We must have peace, you see. But must we? What about righteousness? Was Pilate right? Ekken, one of the greatest of Japanese philosophers remarks that "if a man will not give his life for righteousness he does not know the relative values of righteousness and life." "He dodges trouble," House said about Wilson, long before the war. And because, in the world's evil day, a man like that held his position, millions of people in how many lands use that unhappy soul as the last test of their Christianity. "Forgive us our trespasses," they say, "as we forgive them who have trespassed against us" (Matthew 6:12). And then they pause, and wonder, is that true? Do I forgive the man, but for whose dodging of trouble my boy would have been alive today. And they are not quite sure. Pilate, too, tried to dodge trouble. But you can't. Are we, too, trying that? Are we, too, sinking to that level? What if a day comes when you can't have peace and righteousness? What if the gutters must just run with blood, and our homes again be broken, and our hearts along with them, or Christ be led to Calvary? What then?

The Role of the People

Lastly, there was the people, the kindly, decent, foolish, likable, thoughtless people. For in the end, as always, it was really they who were responsible. It was they who did it; for they could have stopped it. And they had their chance. When Pilate left it to them, no doubt he was quite certain he had found the way to free Christ. For he must have known of the enthusiasm for Him in the streets, of the long roar of rapturous welcome, must have been aware how many in the city Christ had healed, them or their dear ones. There could be no doubt, he must have felt, about the popular verdict. Christ's reprieve was sure. And he was plainly taken aback and disconcerted when there came that long shout for Barabbas, and no single voice for Christ.

It was only a little gathering of course. But where were the others, those on whom Pilate had relied. They must have heard of Christ's arrest and trial, yet they were not there, had not sufficient interest to be there, they who, if they had been there, could have saved

Him. Why did they fail? How did they make themselves responsible for this ghastly horror? Oh well, there were the usual excuses we all make. After all it was no affair of theirs, you know. They were busy sight-seeing; for it was not often they were up in the capital. Some of them, it may even be, had not been there before. They had their friends to look up, and these had detained them. Or they were worshiping in the temple. Or, like enough, they felt there was no need for them to hurry to the court. Christ could not be in any pressing danger. He would be all right. The others would be there to shout for Him. There was no lack of voices yesterday. They need not bother running through the heat. And so, because everyone felt there was no need to be there, Christ died—a perfectly unnecessary death, if only even a few had done their part.

Let us remember that. For is it not just so that things that the world cries for get delayed and frustrated? It is not through ill-will, nor through hostility, but because people can't be bothered voting, or they stay indoors, or are made to feel that they could make no difference, and will never be missed, that changes are not made. Yet we can all do something that would help. Not much perhaps, yet yours, and yours, and yours, and mine, added together, would be quite enough. And it is because these littles we could offer are awanting nothing happens, and the shame goes on. "When I see a poor devil drunk and brutal," said Morris, "I always feel a sort of shame as if I myself had some hand in it." We have. We are responsible. Their blood is upon us and on our children. We are not hostile, we are not indifferent, we are not against it. But we are not there. And so again Christ dies.

So true is it, as Paul cries with eyes glazed with horror, that we, too, you and I, have crucified the Lord of Glory, and have put Him to an open shame. It was not something gross, unthinkable, obscene, that brought Christ to His cross, but little decent sins of ordinary decent people such as we sin every day. Look at your hands, and make sure you have not Christ's blood upon them even now!

NOTES

The Great Attraction: The Uplifted Christ

Reuben Archer Torrey (1856-1928) was one of America's best-known evangelists and Bible teachers. Educated at Yale and various German universities, he went through a time of skepticism from which he emerged a staunch preacher of the faith. In 1889, D.L. Moody called Torrey from the pastorate to become superintendent of his new school in Chicago, now the Moody Bible Institute. He also served as pastor of the Chicago Avenue Church, now the Moody Church. He and Charles Alexander conducted evangelistic meetings together in many parts of the world. From 1912-19, Torrey served as dean of the Bible Institute of Los Angeles. He served from 1914 as pastor of the Church of the Open Door. From 1924 to his death, he ministered in conferences and taught at the Moody Bible Institute.

This sermon is from his book *The Gospel for Today*, published in 1922 by Fleming H. Revell Co.

Reuben Archer Torrey

9

THE GREAT ATTRACTION: THE UPLIFTED CHRIST

And I, if I be lifted up from the earth, will draw all men unto myself (John 12:32).

IN A RECENT advertisement of a Sunday evening service in one of our American cities it was stated that there would be three attractions: a high-class movie show, a popular gospel pianist and his wife, rendered by a well-known prima donna. It is somewhat startling when an unusually gifted and popular preacher, or his advertising committee, thinks of the gospel of the Son of God as having so lost its power to draw, that it must be bolstered up by putting on a selection from a very questionable opera, rendered by a professional opera singer, as an additional attraction to help out our once crucified and now glorified Savior and Lord.

This advertisement set me to thinking as to what really was the great attraction to men in this day as well as in former days? At once there came to my mind the words of our text containing God's answer to this question: "And I, if I be lifted up from the earth, will draw all men unto myself." There is nothing else that draws like the uplifted Christ. Movies may get a crowd of empty-headed and empty-hearted young men and maidens, and even middle-aged folks without brains or moral earnestness, for a time, but nothing really draws and holds the men and women who are worthwhile like Jesus Christ lifted up. Nineteen centuries of Christian history prove the drawing power of Jesus when He is properly presented to men. I have seen some wonderful verification of the assertion of our text as to the marvelous drawing power of the uplifted Christ.

In London, for two continuous months, six afternoons and evenings each week, I saw the great Royal Albert Hall filled and even jammed, and sometimes as many turned away as got in, though it would seat 10,000 people by actual count and stand 2,000 more in the dome. On the opening night of these meetings a leading reporter of the city of London came to me before the service began and said, "You have taken this building for two consecutive months?" "Yes." "And you expect to fill it every day?" "Yes." "Why," he said, "no one has ever attempted to hold two weeks' consecutive meetings here of any kind. Gladstone himself could not fill it for two weeks. And you really expect to fill it for two months?" I replied, "Come and see." He came and he saw.

On the last night, when the place was jammed to its utmost capacity and thousands outside clamored for admission, he came to me again and I said, "Has it been filled?" He smiled and said, "It has." But what filled it? No show on earth could have filled it once a day for many consecutive days. The preacher was no remarkable orator. He had no gift of wit and humor, and would not have exercised it if he had. The newspapers constantly called attention to the fact that he was no orator, but the crowds came and came and came. On both rainy days, and fine days they crowded in or stood outside, oftentimes in a downpour of rain, in the vain hope of getting in. WHAT DREW THEM? The uplifted Christ preached and sung in the power of the Holy Spirit, given in answer to the daily prayers of 40,000 people scattered throughout the earth.

In Liverpool, the Tournament Hall, that was said to seat 20,000 people, and that by actual count seated 12,500 comfortably, located in a very out-of-the-way part of the city, several blocks from the nearest street-car line, and perhaps half a mile from all the regular street-car lines, was filled night after night for three months, and on the last night they crowded 15,000 people into the building at seven o'clock, and then emptied it, and crowded another 15,000 in who had been patiently waiting outside; 30,000 people drawn in a single night! By what? By whom? Not by the preacher, not by the singer, but by Him who had said nearly nineteen hundred years before, "And I, if I be lifted up from the earth, will draw all men unto myself."

The Exact Meaning of the Text

Let us now look at the exact meaning of the text.

First, notice who is the speaker, and what were the circumstances under which He spoke? The Speaker was our Lord Jesus. Not the Christ of men's imaginings, but the Christ of reality, the Christ of actual historic fact. Not the Christ of Mary Baker Eddy's maudlin fancy, or of Madam Besant's mystical imaginings, but the Christ of actuality, who lived here among men and was seen, heard and handled by men, and who was soon to die a real death to save real sinners from a real hell and a real heaven.

The circumstances were these. Certain Greeks among those who went up to worship at the Jewish feast came to one of the apostles, Philip, and said, "We would see Jesus" (John 12:21). And Philip went to Andrew and told Andrew what these Greeks said. Andrew and Philip together came and told Jesus. In the heart-cry of these Greeks, "We would see Jesus," our Lord recognized the yearning of the universal heart, the heart of Greek, as well as Jew, for a satisfying Savior. The Greeks had their philosophers and sages, their would-be satisfiers and saviors, the greatest the world has ever known—Socrates, Aristotle, Plato, Epictetus, Epimenides, and many others—but they did not save, and they did not satisfy, and the Greeks cried, "We would see JESUS." In their eager coming Jesus foresaw the millions of all nations who would flock to Him when He had been crucified as the universal Savior, meeting all the needs of all mankind, and so He cried, "And I, if I be lifted up from the earth, will draw all men unto myself."

In the second place, notice the words, "If I be lifted up." To what does Jesus refer? The next verse answers the question. "But this he said, signifying by what manner of death he should die" (John 12:33). Jesus referred to His lifting up on the cross, to die as an atoning Savior for all mankind. This verse is often quoted as if it meant that, if we lifted up Christ in our preaching, He would draw men. That is true, and it is a crying shame that we do not hold just *Him* up more in our preaching, and we would draw far more people if we did; but that is not our Lord's meaning. The *lifting up* clearly referred not to His not being lifted up by His enemies on the cross, to expose Him to awful shame and to an agonizing death. It is Christ *crucified* who draws; it is Christ crucified who meets the deepest needs of the heart of all mankind. It is an atoning Savior, a Savior who atones for the sins of men by His death, and thus saves from the holy wrath of an infinitely holy God, who meets the needs of men, and thus draws all men, for all men are sinners. Preach any Christ but a crucified Christ, and you will not draw men for long. Preach any gospel but a gospel of atoning blood, and it will not draw for long.

Unitarianism does not draw men. Unitarian churches are born only to die. Their corpses strew New England today. Many of their ministers have been intellectually among the most brilliant our country has ever known, but their churches even under scholarly and brilliant ministers die, die, die. Why? Because Unitarianism presents a gospel *without atoning blood*, and Jesus has said and history has proven it true, "And I, if I be lifted up from the earth, will draw all men unto myself." "Christian Science," strangely so called, for as has been often truly said, "is neither Christian nor scientific," draws crowds of men and women of a certain type, men and women who have or imagine that they have physical ailments, and who will follow anything no matter how absurd, that promises them a little surcease from their real or imagined pains. It also draws crowds who wish to fancy that they have some religion without paying the price of true religion, genuine love, real self-sacrifice, and costly sympathy. But Christian

Science does not draw all men, that is, all kinds and conditions and ranks of men. In fact for the most part it does not draw men at all, but women, and the alleged men it draws are for the most part women in trousers, and men who see any easy way to make a living by preying upon the credulity of luckless females. No, a bloodless gospel, a gospel with a Christ but not a Christ lifted up on a cross, does not meet the universal needs of men, and so does not draw all men.

Congregationalism of late years has been sadly tinctured with Unitarianism. In spite of the fact that it has been an eye-witness to Unitarianism's steady decay and death, Congregationalism has largely dropped the atoning blood out of its theology, and consequently it is rapidly going to the wall. Its once great Andover Seminary, still great in the size of its endowment that was given for the teaching of Bible orthodoxy, but which the conscienceless teachers of a bloodless theology have deliberately taken for the exploitation of their "damnable heresies" (2 Peter 2:1), and which is still great in the number of its professors, graduated at their annual graduating exercises last spring just three men, one a Japanese, one a Hindu, and one an American. A theology without a crucified Savior, without the atoning blood, won't draw. It does not meet the need. No, no, the words of our Lord are still true, "And I, if I be lifted up from the earth, will draw all men unto myself."

Note, in the third place, the words, "Draw all men." Does "all men" mean all individuals or men of all races? Did Jesus mean that every man and woman who lived on this earth would be drawn to Him, or did He mean that men of all races would be drawn to Him? The context answers the question. The Greeks, as we have seen, came to one of the apostles, Philip, and said, "We would see Jesus," and Philip had gone and told Andrew, and Andrew and Philip had gone and told Jesus. Our Lord's ministry during His earthly life was to Jews only, and in the coming of these Greeks so soon before His death, our Lord saw the presage of the coming days when by His death on the cross the barrier between Jews and Gentiles would be broken down and all nations would have their opportunity equally with the Jews, when by His atoning death on the cross men of all nations would be drawn to Him. He did not say that He would draw every individual, but that all races of men: Greeks as well as Jews, Romans, Scythians, French, English, Germans, Japanese, Americans, and men of all nations. He is a universal Savior, and true Christianity is a universal religion. Mohammedanism, Buddhism, Confucianism, and all other religions, but Christianity, are religions of a restricted application. Christianity, with a crucified Christ as its center, is a universal religion that meets the needs of all mankind. It meets the needs of the European as well as the needs of the Asiatic, the needs of the Occident as well as the needs of the Orient, the needs of the American Indian and the needs of the African Negro; and so our Lord said, "And I, if I be lifted up from the earth, will draw all men unto myself."

No race has ever been found anywhere on this earth to which the gospel did not appeal and whose deepest need the crucified Christ did not meet. Many years ago, when Charles Darwin, the eminent English scientist, came in contact with the Terre del Fuegans in their gross degradation, he publicly declared that here was a people to whom it was vain to send missionaries, as the gospel could not do anything for them. But brave men of God went there and took the gospel to them in the power of the Holy Spirit, and demonstrated that it met the need of the Terre del Fuegans, with such great results that Charles Darwin publicly admitted his mistake and became a regular subscriber to the work.

The gospel, *with a crucified Christ as its center*, meets the needs of all conditions and classes of men as well as of all races. It meets the need of the millionaire and the need of the pauper; it meets the need of great men of science like James D. Dana our Lord Kelvin, and the need of the man or woman who cannot read nor write;

it meets the need of the king on the throne and the need of the laborer in the ditch. I myself have seen with my own eyes noblemen and servant girls, university deans and men who could scarcely read, prisoners in penitentiaries and leaders in moral uplift, brilliant lawyers and dull plodding workingmen, come under its attraction, and be saved by its power. But it was only because I made "Christ crucified," His atoning work, the center of my preaching.

Notice in the fourth place, the words "Unto me." "I will draw all men unto me." The Revised Version reads "Unto myself," and that was just what Jesus said, "And I, if I be lifted up from the earth, will draw all men unto myself." It is not to a creed or a system of doctrine that Jesus draws men, but to a Person, to Himself. That is what we need, a *Person*, Jesus Himself. As He Himself once said, "Come unto me, all ye that labor and are heavy laden, and I will give you rest" (Matthew 11:28). Creeds and confessions of faith are all right in their place, they are of great value; the organized church is of great value, it is indispensable, and it is the most important institution in the world today; society would soon go to rack and ruin without it. We are all under solemn obligation to God and to our fellow-man to support the church and belong to it, but creeds and confessions of faith cannot save. The church cannot save. A Divine Person can save, Jesus Christ, and He alone. So He says, "And I, if I be lifted up from the earth, will draw all men unto myself."

Why Christ Lifted Up on the Cross
Draws All Men Unto Himself

But why does Christ lifted up on the cross, the crucified Christ, draw all men unto Himself? There are two reasons why Christ lifted up, and Christ crucified draws all men unto Himself.

First, Christ crucified draws all men unto Himself because Christ crucified meets the first, the deepest, the greatest and most fundamental need of man. What is man's first, greatest, deepest, most fundamental need? A Savior? A Savior from what? First of all, and underlying all else, a Savior from the guilt of sin. Every man of every race has sinned. As Paul put it in Romans 3:22, 23, "There is no difference, for all have sinned and come short of the glory of God." There is no difference between Jew and Gentile, at this point, nor is there any difference between English and German at this point, there is no difference between American and Japanese at this point, no difference between the European and Asiatic, no difference between the American and the African. "There is no difference; for all have sinned and come short of the glory of God."

Every man of every race is a sinner, "there is no difference" at this point. And every man shall have to answer for his sin to the infinitely holy God who rules this universe. Therefore, all men need an atoning Savior who can by His atoning death make propitiation for, and so cover up, our sins—thus reconciling us to this holy God, delivering us from His awful wrath, and bringing us out into the glorious sunlight of His favor. And Jesus lifted up is the only atoning Savior in the universe. He who alone was at the same time God and man, He alone can make atonement for sin. He has made it, has made a perfect atonement, and God has accepted His atonement and testified to His acceptance of His atonement by raising Him from the dead. The Lord Jesus actually meets our need. He actually meets every man's first, greatest, deepest, most fundamental need, and He alone.

In all the universe there is no other religion but Christianity that even offers an atoning Savior. Mohammedanism offers Mohemmed, "The Prophet," a teacher, but not a Savior. Buddhism offers Buddha, supposedly at least a wonderful teacher, "The Light of Asia," but not an atoning Savior. Confucianism offers Confucius, a marvelous teacher far ahead of his time, but not an atoning Savior. No religion offers an atoning Savior, offers an atonement of any real character, but

Christianity. This is the radical point of difference between Christianity and every other religion in the world, yet some fool preachers are trying to eliminate from Christianity this, its very point of radical difference from all other religions. But such an emasculated Christianity will not reach the needs of men and will not draw men. It never has and it never will.

The Bible and history are at one at this point. Jesus Christ offers Himself lifted up on the cross to redeem us from the curse of the law, by "becoming a curse in our behalf." "Christ hath redeemed us from the curse of the law, being made a curse for us; for it is written, Cursed is every one that hangeth on a tree" (Galatians 3:13). Men know their need; they may try to forget it, they may try to deny it, they may try to drown their sense of it by drink and dissipation or by wild pleasure-seeking or wild money-getting, or by listening to fake preachers in supposedly orthodox pulpits, like one who in this city declared recently that, "the old sense of sin is fast disappearing," and added, "the change is for the better not for the worse." He spoke also of "imaginary and artificial sins like 'the sin of unbelief'," and then went on to say, "In this we agree with Christ," apparently not knowing enough about the Bible to know that Jesus Himself was the very one who said in John 16:8, 9, "And he, when he is come, will convict the world in respect of sin, and of righteousness, and of judgment; of sin, because they believe not on me."

But in spite of all our attempts to drown or stupefy or silence our sense of sin, our consciousness of guilt before a Holy God, we all have it, and like Banquo's Ghost, it will not down. Nothing gives the guilty conscience abiding peace but the atoning blood of Jesus Christ. And so, Christ *lifted up* draws all men unto Him, and even wicked ministers of Satan, like the preacher I have just referred to, sometimes come to their senses and flee to the real Christ, Christ *crucified*, as I hope this one may. Yes, Jesus, Jesus only, Jesus lifted up on the cross, Jesus crucified for our sins, making full atonement for our sins, He and He alone meets the deepest need of us all, and so His cross draws us all unto Himself. Happy the man or the woman who yields to that drawing; woe be to the man or woman who resists that drawing; final gloom, despondency, and despair are their lot. Oh, how many men and women who have gotten their eyes opened to see the facts, to see their awful guilt, and who have been plunged into deepest consequent despair, have come to me, and I have pointed them to *Jesus on the cross* and have shown them by God's Word all their sins laid upon Him and thus settled. They have come to Him and believed God's testimony about Him, that He had borne all their sins in His own body on the cross, and they have found perfect peace and boundless joy. And that is the only way to find perfect peace and boundless joy.

Will you set out to find peace? If you do not, great gloom and utter despair, await you some day, in this world or in the world to come. In my first pastorate I tried to get a man to come to *Christ lifted up* to meet his need of pardon. Though this was many years ago, he held to the theology that is preached as "new theology" today. He sought to still the voice of conscience and stupefy his sense of sin by denying his guilt and his need of an atoning Savior. He did not wish to listen to me nor to see me. But the hour came when death drew nigh. A cancer was eating its way through scalp and skull into his brain; then he cried to those about his dying bed, "Send for Mr. Torrey." I hurried to his side. He was in despair. "Oh!" he said, "Dr. Tidhall tells me that I have but a short time to live, that as soon as this cancer gets a little further and eats through the thin film of skull and touches the brain I am a dead man. Tell me how to be saved."

I tried to make as plain as I knew how the way of salvation through the uplifted Christ, Christ uplifted on the cross, and I think I know how to make it plain, but he had waited too long, he could not grasp it. I stayed with him. Night came on. I said to his family, "You have been up night after night with him, I will sit with him tonight." They instructed me what to do, how to minister to him. Time after time during the night I had to go to another room to get some nourishment for him, and as I would come back into the room where he lay, from his bed in the corner there would rise the constant cry, "Oh, I wish I were a Christian. Oh, I wish I were a Christian. Oh, I wish I were a Christian." And thus he died.

In the second place, Christ lifted up on the cross, Christ crucified draws all men unto Him, because lifted up there to die for us He reveals His wonderful love, and the wondrous love of the Father for us. "Hereby know we the love of God, because he laid down his life for us" (1 John 3:16), and "God commendeth his love toward us, in that while we were yet sinners, Christ died for us" (Romans 5:6, 8). There is nothing that draws men like love. Love draws all men in every clime. But no other love draws like the love of God. John 3:16, "For God so loved the world that he gave his only begotten Son, that whosoever believeth in him should not perish, but have everlasting life," has broken thousands of hard hearts.

One night, preaching in my own church in Minneapolis, the whole choir stayed for the after-meeting. The leading soprano was an intelligent young woman, but she was living a worldly life. She remained with the rest. In the after-meeting, her mother arose in the back of the church and said, "I wish you would pray for the conversion of my daughter." I did not look around but knew instinctively that her cheeks were flushing, and her eyes were flashing with anger. As soon as the meeting was dismissed, I hurried down so that I would meet her before she got out of the church. As she came toward me I held out my hand to her. She stamped her foot, and with flashing eyes cried, "Mr. Torrey, my mother knows better than to do that. She knows it will only make me worse." I said, "Sit down, Cora." She sat down, and without any argument I opened my Bible to Isaiah 53:5, and began to read, "But he was wounded for our transgressions; he was bruised for our iniquities; the chastisement of our peace was upon him; and with his stripes we are healed." She burst into tears, and the next night accepted Jesus Christ. I had to go to Duluth for a few days, and when I returned I found that she was seriously ill. One morning her brother came hurrying up to my home and said that she was apparently dying, that she was unconscious and white from the loss of blood. I hastened down. As I entered the room, she lay there with her eyes closed, with the whitest face I ever saw on one who was not actually dead. She was apparently unconscious, scarcely breathing. I knelt by her side to pray, more for the sake of the mother who stood beside the bed than for her, for I supposed that she was beyond help or hearing. But no sooner had I finished my prayer, than in a clear, full, richly musical tone she began to pray. These were about her words, "Heavenly Father, if it be Thy will, raise me up that as I have used my voice for myself and only to please myself, I may use my voice for Thy glory, but if in Thy wisdom Thou seest that it is best for me not to live, I shall be glad to go to be with Christ," and she went to be with Christ.

Oh, I have seen thousands melted as I have repeated to them and shown them the picture of Christ on the cross, as told in Isaiah 53:5, "But he was wounded for our transgressions; he was bruised for our iniquities; the chastisement of our peace was upon him; and with his stripes we are healed."

A few days ago I received a missionary magazine containing a testimony from one who was going to Egypt under the Egypt General Mission. This young missionary said, "When I was twelve years old, during the Torrey-Alexander meetings, in 1904, I gave my heart to the Lord Jesus Christ. Dr. Torrey was speaking on the text, Isaiah 53:5, and he asked us to repeat the words with him, but changing the word 'our' into the word 'my.' While repeating the text in this way I suddenly realized, as if for the first time, that Jesus had really suffered all this for me, and there and then I gave my life to Him."

Oh! men and women, look now! See Jesus Christ lifted up on the cross, see Him hanging on that awful cross, see Him wounded for your transgressions, bruised for your iniquities, and the chastisement of your peace laid on Him. Oh, men and women living in sin, men and women rejecting Christ for the world, men and women who have looked to the lies of Christian Science, Unitarianism and other systems that deny His atoning blood, Listen! "But he was wounded for our transgressions; he was bruised for our iniquities; the chastisement of our peace was upon him; and with his stripes we are healed."

Won't you yield to that love, won't you give up your sin, give up your worldly pleasures, give up your willful errors, and accept the Savior who loves you and died for you, who was "wounded for your transgressions; bruised for your iniquities" and upon whom the chastisement of your peace was laid? Accept Him right now.

The Logic of the Cross

William Henry Biederwolf (1867-1939) served effectively
as an evangelist, Bible teacher, and educator. He
teamed up with J. Wilbur Chapman for three years,
and in 1924 made a world tour with musician Homer
Rodeheaver. In 1922 Biederwolf became director of the
Winona Lake (Indiana) Bible Conference. He was also
director and later president of the Winona Lake School
of Theology. He spent his last ten years as pastor of
the Royal Poinciana Chapel, Palm Beach, Florida.

This sermon is from his book *Frozen Assets and Other
Sermons*, published in 1933 by William B. Eerdmans
Publishing Company.

William Henry Biederwolf

THE LOGIC

He saved others, Himself He cannot save (........

WHEN THESE WORDS were spoken, the last scene in the earthly life of the Son of God was about over. A few moments more, and as the curtain fell, He cried, "It is finished," and the wrath of the Jewish nation had filled up the cup of the Savior's suffering.

Only a few hours before, He had entered Jerusalem amid the shout of Hosannas and the waving of palms, but scarcely had the branches time to wither in the streets than the cry "HAIL" was turned to "CRUCIFY." Upon Him who was the world's best friend—who might have been a King of realms celestial—was laid the Hebrew criminal cross, that He might bear it away to the place of His death. There while heaven's chorus was hushed and the song of rapture stilled and angels stood with bated breath, the Lamb of God was lifted up to take away the sin of the world.

One would expect that when the malice of the Jews had so far spent itself, that it would be satisfied to let the man Jesus die in peace, or that it would accord to Him at least the same feeling of consideration that the instinct of humanity gives to the poorest dying criminal. But it was not so, for around the Silent Sufferer surged the brutal slaughter and flung its showers of barbed sarcasm in His holy face. The Prisoner has become the sport of the executioners.

The gospels tell us that they who passed by reviled Him, wagging their heads. These passersby were attending the Passover Feast at Jerusalem, and they were no doubt among the number who had only the day before welcomed the Savior into the city of David with loud hosannas. One day it was popular to cheer;

xt to jeer. So fluctuating with the Savior's
uating fortunes, they add their sting to His
proach and spit their venom at Him as they pass.

Little dreaming that within three days He would
rebuild the temple they were then destroying, they wag
their heads and say, "Aha, Thou that destroyest the
temple and rebuildest it in three days, save thyself; if
Thou art the Son of God, come down from the cross."

And the Jewish dignitaries—although they despised
the mob, they despised the Son of God more. From the
river Jordan to Pilate's courtroom they had tracked
Him like a tiger thirsting for His blood, and now, in
this their moment of seeming triumph, they gathered
around His cross to watch Him die, and to taunt Him
with, "Physician, heal thyself" (Luke 4:23). Like the
blind rabble, little knowing that although it was Satan's
greatest triumph, it was at the same time Satan's
greatest defeat, they exult in the powerlessness of
Christ to leave the cross, and with curled lips they cry,
"He saved others, Himself He cannot save."

I think the pain of the thorn-pierced brow and the
spear-riven side and the lacerated limbs must have
been little, if not forgotten, when compared with the
cruel taunts and bitter jests that went like cold steel
into the Savior's bosom. The cruel spikes had pierced
his hands, but these were the nails that pierced His
heart.

"He saved others; Himself He cannot save."

First, let's examine the sense in which these words
were untrue; or, the false limitation of the Savior's
power.

Second, we shall look at the sense in which these
words were true; or, the Savior's inability to furnish
demonstration of a moral impossibility.

And third, we shall study the significance of it all for
you and me.

The Sense in Which the Words Were Untrue

It was a false limitation of the Savior's power. We

have no sympathy with the suggestion that in their minds lay a faint hope that He would descend and thus give them positive proof that He was the Messiah. True, they said, "If thou art the Son of God, come down from the cross. . . . and we will believe" (Matthew 27:40, 42). But, NO, they would not believe. The same hearts that were hardened at the resurrection of Lazarus, and which later refused to believe at the greater miracle of His own resurrection, would not have believed at the instance of this miracle for which they clamored, but were beyond the reach of any external evidence. By the prophecy He fulfilled, by the doctrine He taught, by the life He lived, by the miracles He performed, He had proved that He was the Son of God, and this request of the Jews was only the harbinger of modern infidelity spending itself against the light of truth.

Because He would not, they said He could not. They ought to have known that the same power that made it possible for Him to save others, could now make it possible for Him to save Himself.

But none are so blind as those who refuse to see. They argued thus: "He is not the Son of God, and therefore He must die;" and now they say, "He dies, and therefore He is not the Son of God." And so, not understanding the mystery of love before which they stood, they argued that His present helpless state blows to atoms His pretentions to save others. As the Greek word signified, with curled lips and inflated nostrils, they mean to say, "He pretended to save others; now see, He cannot even save Himself!" And thus, because He would not help Himself, the help He had given to others was branded as a lie.

But was it true? Had He not saved others? It is now time for the witnesses to speak. SPEAK, Bartimaeus, Blind man of Capernaum, Lepers of Samaria, Demoniacs of Gadara, Lazarus. SPEAK and say if He has not saved others.

And how about Himself? One word from His almighty lips and every hand that was lifted up to do Him harm would have been paralyzed. Angels and archangels and all the mighty hosts of heaven stand ready to do His bidding; but He bids them stay. Michael draws His sword; and in fancy I can hear him say, "Son of God, if you want us to come, just take your hand away from the bloody spike—you can do it easily—and give us the signal; just nod your head," but Jesus said, "No."

They tried to murder Him one day, but He vanished from their very presence; so now it would have been a miracle of no greater improbability to have left the cross. Could He have accomplished in any other way the purpose for which He allowed Himself to be nailed upon it? He doubtless would have descended and thus have branded as false forever the limitation put upon His power by the frenzied mob which gathered round His death. And so in the full consciousness of His own eternal power, He turns their "Cannot" into His own "Will not," and bows His head and dies.

Because He would not, is no proof that He could not; but if He could and would not, it is positive evidence that there was some purpose in His staying.

In What Sense the Words of the Scribes Were True

"He saved others; Himself He cannot save." Why did Jesus stay on the cross? Unconsciously the words of this verse bore witness to a mighty truth, and by their words they made a garland of imperishable beauty to wreath around the Savior's brow. It was indeed most true. If He would save others, He could not save Himself. And thus the cross becomes the throne of His saving power.

It was morally impossible for Christ to leave the cross. He was the Mediator for you and me, He was the pledged surety, and the Jews demanded such a demonstration as involved a moral impossibility in its execution. If He would bear away the sin of the world, He must pay the penalty of the world's sin. God's great plan of salvation was well nigh consummated; the Lamb for the necessary sacrifice had been brought to the altar, and at this critical point they say, "If thou art the Son of God, come down from the cross." They challenged Him to save Himself from the cross while He was saving others by the cross. This thing He could not do. But one thing remained to be done, and the world's redemption would be finished. This one thing they challenge Him not to do.

The earth quaked and the sky grew dark when He died. It seems as though the heart of the earth broke and the heavens put on mourning. But whatever may have been the meaning of those mysterious signs, it would have been dark indeed had He accepted their challenge and left the cross and left the world one day to awake out of its night of sin into the deeper darkness of everlasting shame and contempt. To have descended from the cross would have been to falsify every Old Testament prediction, every rite and sacrifice; to have repudiated His own teaching; to brand His every miracle; to thwart the eternal plan of His Father in heaven; and to have left the world unredeemed forever.

But He did not come down. He died that you and I might live. He was stripped that you and I might be robed. He accepted thorns that you and I might wear crowns. He was cast out of the city of David that you and I might enter into the New Jerusalem, the city of God. If we would but be silent now, I think we might hear Him in accents low and tender:

> I gave my life for Thee; my precious blood I shed,
> That thou might'st ransomed be, and quickened from
> the dead.
> And I have suffered much, more than thy tongue can
> tell,
> Of bitterest agony, to rescue thee from hell.

The Significance of It for You and Me

If you are not a Christian, it means the very best that heaven could do was done to save you from your sin.
I have read somewhere the story of a man who fell

from a high scaffolding and of another below who reached out his arms to catch him. The falling man was scarcely injured, but when he struck his savior the force of the fall drove his arms into sockets, broke his shoulder, frightfully pushed his spine out of shape and caused him to go deformed forever. After months of awful suffering, he rose from his bed to walk the streets an object of pity to everyone who met him. One day he was asked what had become of the man whom he had saved; and what kind of a look do you suppose came over his face? It brightened, and he said, "He gave half of his property to his rescuer; he divides his earnings with me now, and never allows me for a moment to be in want." Ah, there is something that men know how to appreciate. But suppose he had forgotten him. Suppose he had turned away from him when he met him on the street and refused to recognize his obligation to him? I know what you would say. And yet there are some of you who seem to forget that there is One who was maimed and bruised and crushed and broken for you, who put Himself between you and death and who has been kept waiting all these years for just a word of thanks, or a look of grateful recognition.

If you are a Christian, it means that there must live and rule in your life the spirit which lived and ruled in His.

"Come down from the cross and save Thyself," they said to Jesus. But Jesus had no place in His program for the saving of Himself. Among the last things He said as He was going up to Jerusalem to die, was, "Except a grain of wheat fall into the ground and die, it abideth by itself alone. But if it die—if it die, it bringeth forth much fruit" (John 12:24). He used this illustration to show the necessity of His death and it explains why He calmly breathed out His life on the cross while the crowd below was taunting Him because He was dying. And the same principle must control your life and mine if we are to meet the divine requirement as to what life is really meant to be.

What a strange and distorted idea of life some people

have! Even the Christian life has been misunderstood by some whom the world has been pleased to number among its holiest of men. They have thought they could best live that life in the seclusion of a mountain cave or a monastery cell, out of touch with and unmindful of the confused and distracted world round about them so full of heartache and of need.

Cloistered visions and mountain-top experiences may enrich the soul, but the vision dims and the blessing will not stay if heavenly experience is not translated into earnest service for a needy humanity. After all, this is where Christ was always found.

> The village priest of austerity
> Climbed up in a high church steeple;
> To be nearer God, so that he might
> Hand His word down to the people.

> And so in sermon script he daily wrote
> What he thought came from heaven;
> And dropped it down on the people's heads
> Two times one day in seven.

> In his age God cried, "Come down and die,"
> And he cried from out the steeple,
> "Where art Thou, Lord," and the Lord replied,
> "Down here among my people."

All too much we fail to realize the place that self-sacrifice and service hold in the religion of Jesus Christ. They are the very heart of it. They are the religion of Jesus Christ. Christ's whole existence, all the way from heaven to earth and back again by way of Calvary, was a continual outpouring of Himself for the sake of others. And He says, "If any man will be my disciple, let him take up his cross and follow me" (Mark 8:34).

They tell us that one time in Liverpool a great building was on fire. The flames leaped from every quarter, and dense smoke was blackening the sky above. Suddenly two men appeared in the upper story of the building at one of the windows. Ladder after ladder was brought, but they all fell short, and the longest one was too short by almost a story. The crowd below waited in breathless suspense while the men above stared with pale and ghastly faces into what seemed their certain death. Just then a man past fifty, but brave and strong, stepped out from the crowd. Taking one of the shorter ladders in his hand, he climbed to the top of the one leaning against the building, and raising the short ladder above him on his shoulders, he steadied it with his hands and securing his place as best he could, he cried from his strained position: "Men, come down over me; come down over me." And as the crowd below sent up cheer upon cheer, down over the first ladder the two men came and over the body of the man who held it and on in safety to the ground. Then their savior sank back exhausted from his dizzy height and fell—crushed and bleeding and broken—at their feet.

Oh, men and women, this is the significance of the cross for you and me. When the Roman soldier took the oath to live and to suffer and to die for Rome, he raised his hand when the oath was read and said, "This for me; This for me."

Oh, that God this morning might smite the self, the pride, and the unholy ambition of our souls. If we have not gone up to Calvary, if our life is not an interpretation of the cross today, then let us this day, this very hour, go up to Jerusalem and out to that hill not far away and stretch out our hands in the place where the hate and the selfishness of the world pierced His, and there ask God to begin at once to drive the nails that shall cause us to die forever unto self and live forever unto Him.

> Self is the only prison that can ever bind the soul,
> Love is the only angel who can bid the gates unroll;
> And when He comes to call thee, arise and follow fast;
> His way may lie through darkness, but it leads to light
> at last.

NOTES

The Cross and the World

George H. Morrison (1866-1928) assisted the great
Alexander Whyte in Edinburgh, pastored two churches,
and then became pastor in 1902 of the distinguished
Wellington Church on University Avenue in Glasgow.
His preaching drew crowds; in fact, people had to line
up an hour before the services to be sure to get seats in
the large auditorium. Morrison was a master of
imagination in preaching, yet his messages were solidly
biblical.

From his many published volumes of sermons, I have
chosen this message, found in *The Weaving of Glory*,
published by Hodder and Stoughton, London.

George H. Morrison

11

THE CROSS AND THE WORLD

I am not sent but to the lost sheep of the house of Israel (Matthew 15:24).

I, if I be lifted up, will draw all men unto Me (John 12:32).

ALL WE HAVE to do is read the record of the gospels to find confirmation of the first of these two verses. The whole activity of Christ on earth shows Him as sent to the lost sheep of Israel. Within the boundaries of Israel He was born, and within the boundaries of Israel He died. With the one exception of the journey here recorded, He never in His maturity left the Jewish land. His twelve disciples were of the Jewish faith; His friends were inhabitants of Jewish homes; His enemies were not the Romans, but His own, to whom He came and they received Him not. For His teaching He sought no other audience than the men and women of the Jewish villages. For His retirement He sought no other solitude than the solitude of the Galilean hills. All His miracles, with certain rare exceptions, which were recorded because they were exceptional, were wrought for the comforting of Jewish hearts and for the drying of tears in Jewish eyes. The whole story of the gospel, then, is a witness to the truth of our first text. In the fulfilling of his earthly ministry, Christ confined Himself to Jewish limits. He did so because of His assurance, reached in ways we cannot now consider, that He was sent to the lost sheep of the house of Israel.

As we study the words of our Redeemer, one thing gradually grows very clear. He anticipated a ministry that should be wider than these Jewish limits. I am not thinking just now of any words He spoke after He was risen from the dead. I am thinking only of His recorded utterances in those crowded years before the cross. What I say is that no reasonable man can study the discourse of the historic Jesus without discovering that He foresaw a ministry which was to be as wide as the whole world. There is, for instance, the second of our texts today—"I will draw all men unto Me." There is that beautiful word of an earlier chapter, "Other sheep I have which are not of this fold" (John 10:16). There is that utterance at Simon's table, when the woman broke the alabaster box, "Wheresoever this gospel shall be preached in the whole world, this that she hath done shall be told of her" (Matthew 26:13). Observe that these great sayings have stood the test of the most searching criticism. They are so germane to the mind of Christ that they have come triumphant through the fires. And they tell us this: Through His earthly ministry, confined as it was within the house of Israel, Christ had the outlook of an approaching lordship over the nations of mankind.

But these utterances tell us more than that, and to this I invite your attention. They tell us that in the mind of Jesus His death and His worldwide empire were related. So far as we can learn the mind of Christ, we can with reverence say this about it. It was when the cross was clearest in His thought that the worldwide empire was most clear to Him. If you will think of the texts I have cited and consider the occasion of their utterance, you will understand quite easily what I mean.

Take for instance that most beautiful word, "Other sheep I have which are not of this fold" (John 10:16). What are the words that precede it? "The good shepherd giveth his life for the sheep" (John 10:11). At the very moment when the thought of shepherding kindled the vision of the shepherd's death, there flashed upon the Lord the vision of the sheep beyond the fold. Take again the scene at Simon's feast where Jesus spoke of a gospel for the world. "Wheresoever this gospel shall be preached in the whole world, there this deed that she hath done shall be remembered" (Matthew 26:13).

And what was it that the woman had done under the interpreting eyes of Jesus Christ? She had anointed His body for its burial. In other words that womanly act of hers had spoken to Jesus of His coming death. Over the table where the guests reclined, it had cast the awful shadow of the cross. And it was then, anointed for His burial by an act which no one else could understand, that Christ in vision lifted up His eyes and saw the gospel preached to the whole world. Clearly Christ looked upon His death as the great secret of a worldwide empire. When the one grew vivid in His thought, there rose on Him the vision of the other. And that to me is a matter to be brooded on, as one of the most momentous of all truths, by every man and every woman who is interested in the world-empire of the Lord. Now the question is this: Can we follow out that thought and see even dimly where the connection lies? It is that which I should like to attempt to do in this message.

Christ's Death: The Motive for Missions

In the first place, it is the death of Christ which supplies the motive of missionary enterprise.

We must always remember that when we speak of the death of Christ, we speak of a death different from our own. Our death is the cessation of activity: Christ's was the crown and climax of His life. "I have power to lay it down" (John 10:18), He said, and that is a power no other man has shared. We die when our appointed hour comes. When the hand of God hath touched us, we sleep. But Christ never looked upon His death like that, as something inevitable and irresistible. He looked on it as the last free glorious service of a life that had always been a life of love. Here in one gleam, intense and vivid, was gathered up the light of all His years. Here in one action, which we name His dying, was gathered up the love in which He wrought. And it is just because of the power of that action, concentrating all the scattered rays, that Christ could say, "I, if I be lifted up, will draw all men unto Me."

How true this is as a fact of history we see in the story of the Christian church. There is the closest connection in that story between the death of Christ and missionary zeal. There have been periods in the church's history when the death of Christ was practically hidden. The message of the cross was rarely preached; the meaning of the cross was rarely grasped. The gospel was looked on as a refined philosophy, eminently fitted for the good of men, inculcating a most excellent morality, and in perfect harmony with human reason. We have had periods like that in Scotland and in England. God grant that they may never come again with their deadening of true religion. And always when you have such a period, when love is nothing and moral law is everything, you have a period when not a hand is lifted for the salvation of the heathen world. For it is not morality that seeks the world; it is religion centering in love. It is a view of a divine love so wonderful that it stooped to the service of death on a cross. So always, in evangelical revival, when that has been apprehended in the wonder of it, the passion to tell it out has come again, and men have carried the message to mankind.

May I say that it is along these lines that the road must lie to a deepening of interest. To realize what it means that Christ has died is to have a gospel that we must impart. There are many excellent people who, in their secret heart, confess to a very faint interest in missions. They give, and it may be they give generously and yet in their hearts they know that they are not interested. They know nothing about mission fields, they never go to missionary meetings, and they take the opportunity to visit a sister church when a missionary is advertised to preach in theirs. With such people I have no lack of sympathy, for I think I understand their position thoroughly. I have the gravest doubt if any good is done by trying excitedly to lash up their interest. But I am perfectly confident that these good people would waken to a new and lively interest, if only they realized a little more the wonder of the love of God in Christ.

What do you think is the most wonderful thing that ever happened? It is not the kindling of the myriad stars, nor the fashioning of the human eye that it might see them. It is that once the God who is eternal stooped down from heaven, came into humanity, bore our burdens, carried our sorrows, and died in redeeming love upon the tree. Once you realize what that means, everything else in the world is insignificant. Once you realize what that means, you must pass it on to other people. And that is the source of missionary zeal, not blind obedience, nor any thoughts of terror, but the passing on of news so wonderful that we cannot—dare not—keep it to ourselves.

Christ's Death: The Universal Longing Answered

In the next place, the death of Christ interprets and answers a universal longing. It meets with perfect satisfaction the deepest need of all the world.

One of the great gains of our age is that it has drawn the world together. There is an intermingling of the nations that but a few decades ago was quite impossible. Thanks to the means of transport, and to the need of expansion on the part of nations; thanks to the deathless spirit of adventure, to the gains of commerce and to the march of armies, there is a blending now of the whole earth such as was undreamed of once. One result of all that intermingling has been a new sense of the oneness of humanity. No longer do we delight in travelers' tales, such as captivated the Middle Ages. Men push their way into untraveled forests, and they come to us from Arabia and Tibet, and under all that is strange they bring us tidings of the touch of nature that makes the whole world kin. We realize today as men had never done, how God made all nations of one blood. Deeper than everything that separates, there are common sorrows and elemental hopes. There is one common heart by which we live; one common life in which we share; one common enemy awaiting all, when the pitcher is broken at the fountain.

But especially has this oneness of humanity been made evident in the religious life. That has been one incalculable gain of the study of comparative religion. It has investigated a thousand rites and found at the back of them a common longing. It has touched the foundations of a thousand altars, and found they were built upon a common need. It has gathered from Africa, from India, from China, the never-failing story of religion, and always at the very heart of things it has discovered one unchanging element. It is not enough to say that all men have religion. That is now an accepted thing.

Something far more wonderful and thrilling has been slowly emerging into prominence. It is that under a thousand different rites, from those of Patagonia to those of China, there lies the unquenchable desire of man to get into right relationship with God. Deeper than all sense of gratitude, though gratitude is very often there—deeper than unreasoning terror, though heathen religion is always big with terror—deeper than that, this fact stands out today, based on exhaustive and scientific study: *The deepest longing in the soul of man is the longing to get right with God.* It is that in the last analysis which explains sacrifice, and where is the heathen tribe that does not sacrifice? It is that which explains the sway of heathen witchcraft, of which the evils can never be exaggerated. The religious life is the deepest life of man, and in that life, over the whole wide world, the one determining and vital question is this—how can mortal man get right with God?

I almost ask your pardon for having taken you so far afield. But you see, I think, the point which I am driving at, and from which there is no possible escape. That very question, so vital to humanity, is the question which the atonement answers. It answers the cry that is rising to the heavens from every heathen rite and heathen altar. It tells men in language that a child can grasp—yet with a depth that angels cannot fathom—how sinful man, by an appointed sacrifice, can be put right with the eternal God. I believe with all my soul in educational missions, but at the heart of missions is more than education. I believe with all my soul in medical missions, but at the heart of missions there is more than healing. Christ never said, "My teaching shall draw all men," nor yet, "My healing power shall draw all men;" He said, "I, if I be lifted up, shall draw all men, and this spake He of the death that He should die." This means that in the atoning death lies the answer to man's deepest need. It means that the deepest cry of all humanity is answered in the message of the cross. And I venture to say that everything we have learned today in the modern study of comparative religion, corroborates, authenticates, and seals that certainty upon the lips of Jesus.

Christ's Death: His Influence Liberated

Then, finally, we have the thought that the death of Christ has liberated His influence. It has opened the window of the ark, if I might put it so, that the dove might fly abroad over the waters. "It is expedient for you that I go away," He said, "for if I go not away the Comforter cannot come" (John 16:7). Now the Lord is that Spirit, says the apostle—it is that same Jesus glorified and liberated. So by the lifting up on the cross, Christ was set free from local limitation, to pass into a spiritual ministry that should be co-extensive with the world. No longer can any village of far Galilee claim the present monopoly of Christ. No longer can loving hearts in Bethany say, "He is our guest and ours only for tonight." He is as present now by the lake shores of Africa as He is within this house of God this evening, and present so because He lived and died.

We talk of the story of the cross as if in that story lay the world's redemption. I beg you to remember that while that is true, it is far from being all the truth. Christ spoke not a word of the story of the cross. He said, I—persisting through the cross—I, the living Christ, will draw the world—I whom death is powerless to hold. In other words, when our missionaries go forth, they go with something more than a sweet story. They go with Him of whom the tale is told, so wonderful, so unspeakable, so moving. They go with Him who, having tasted death, is now alive and lives forevermore, and who is able to save unto the uttermost all who come unto God by Him.

The Darkness of Golgotha

George Campbell Morgan (1863-1945) was the son of a British Baptist preacher and preached his first sermon when he was 13 years old. He had no formal training for the ministry, but his tireless devotion to the study of the Bible helped him to become one of the leading Bible teachers of his day. Rejected by the Methodists, he was ordained into the Congregational ministry. He was associated with Dwight L. Moody in the Northfield Bible conferences and as an itinerant Bible teacher. He is best known as the pastor of Westminster Chapel, London (1904-17 and 1933-45). During his second term there, he had Dr. D. Martyn Lloyd-Jones as his associate.

He published more than 60 books and booklets, and his sermons are found in *The Westminster Pulpit* (London, Pickering and Inglis). This sermon is from Volume 7.

12

THE DARKNESS OF GOLGOTHA

From the sixth hour there was darkness over all the land until the ninth hour (Matthew 27:45).

THERE'S ALWAYS THE danger that we might read this verse too quickly. We treat it too often as though it were merely the record of something incidental.

As a matter of fact, it is the central verse in the story of the cross. Indeed, the cross itself is not mentioned in the verse—no word is spoken of it or of the Christ. They are alike hidden, and yet the period was one of three hours' duration, the very central hours of the experience of the Savior of men. Christ and the cross are alike hidden within that verse, and that fact is most suggestive because in those hours transactions were accomplished that through all eternity defy the apprehension and explanation of finite minds.

It is not to be passed over lightly that all the Synoptists record the fact of that darkness. Three hours of darkness and of silence! All the ribald clamor was over, the material opposition utterly exhausted, the turmoil ended. Man had done his last and his worst. Beyond that period of the three hours' silence, even human actions were expressive of pity. Nothing has impressed my own heart, or amazed me more in reading this story anew, and attempting to meditate upon it in view of this service, than what I shall venture to describe as the wonderful psychological conditions of those hours beyond the hours of silence.

It is as though that appalling silence and that overwhelming darkness had changed the entire attitude of man to the Savior. The very vinegar they offered Him to drink was offered Him in pity. What they said about Elijah was expressive of their desire to sympathize. The centurion's testimony was that of a man whose heart was strangely moved toward the august and dignified Savior. When presently they found Him dead, and therefore did not break His bones, the spear thrust was one of kindness, lest perchance He might still suffer, in spite of the fact that He appeared to be dead. Multitudes dispersed from the scene at Golgotha smiting their breasts, overwhelmed with a sense of awe, and strangely moved by some new pity. And there is no picture in all the New Testament more full of pathos and of power than that of the women standing silent and amazed through all those hours of His suffering, and still standing there beyond them.

Then also all of the cries that passed the lips of Jesus beyond the darkness were significant. "My God! My God, why didst Thou forsake Me!" (Matthew 27:46)—for that was the tense; a slight change from the tense of the actual Psalm, a question asked by One who was emerging from the experience to which He referred. And then as John is most careful to record for us, "Knowing that all things were now finished, He said, I thirst" (John 19:28). Beyond that came the words of the great proclamation, "It is finished" (John 19:30). And as last the words of the final committal, full of dignity, were spoken: "Father, into Thy hands I commend My spirit" (Luke 23:46). Everything was changed beyond the hours of silence and of darkness.

Much has been written about these hours of darkness, much which is not warranted by any careful spiritual attention to the story itself. You will call to mind how, at great length many years ago, it was argued that the darkness was that of the sun's eclipse. But that is entirely impossible, for Passover was always held at full moon, when there could be no eclipse of the sun. The darkness has been described as nature's sympathy with the suffering of the Lord, but that is a pagan conception of nature, a conception of nature as having some consciousness apart from God and out of harmony with His work. It has been said that the darkness was brought about by an act of God, and was expressive of

His sympathy with His Son. I admit that that is an appealing idea, and has some element of truth in it, in that we may discover the overruling of His government; but to declare that that darkness was caused by God because of His sympathy with His Son is to deny the cry of Jesus which immediately followed the darkness and referred to it. The darkness was to Him a period when He experienced whatever He may have meant by the words, "Thou didst forsake Me" (Matthew 27:46).

If I have succeeded in these words spoken in reverent spirit, in suggesting to you the difficulty of those central three hours, then our hearts are prepared for going forward.

I submit thoughtfully that no interpretation of that darkness is to be trusted save that of the Lord who experienced it. Has He flung any light on the darkness which will enable us to apprehend the meaning of the darkness? Did any word escape His lips that will help us to explain those silent hours? I think the answer is to be found in these narratives, and to that teaching of the Lord we appeal in order that we may consider the meaning of the darkness, and the passing of the darkness, and thereafter attempt reverently to look back at the transaction in the darkness.

The Meaning of the Darkness

What was this darkness? How was it caused? What did it really mean? That this question is of importance is proved by that to which I have already drawn your attention, the fact that Matthew, Mark, and Luke alike carefully record that it took place at this very time. The reference is made by each of them in detail. It was something to be noted, something to be remembered, something that made its impression alike on the evangelist who saw the King, the evangelist who saw the Servant, and the evangelist who saw the Perfect Man. We cannot pass it over as though it were merely incidental, and consequently we shall attempt to discover its meaning in the light of what our Lord Himself said before He passed into the darkness.

Luke records for us a fact not mentioned by either of the other evangelists, that in Gethsemane Jesus said to the man who came to arrest Him, "This is your hour, and the power of darkness" (Luke 22:53). That was a most suggestive word, spoken as I have reminded you, in Gethsemane before He passed from the garden to and through those trial scenes with which you are familiar. After the High Priest cast the incense on the fire and just as He was leaving the garden, Jesus spoke to the men about Him, "This is your hour, and the power of darkness." This is your hour! I go back to this phrase again, not to tarry at length with it, but to ask you most carefully to ponder it.

At the beginning of our Lord's public ministry, He referred to an hour which was not yet, to an hour which was postponed. During the course of His ministry, you will find that the evangelists more than once allude to the same hour, and to that hour, whatever it might have been, as to a postponed hour. Men attempted to arrest Him, but they could not because His hour was not yet come. Men desired to encompass His death, and wrought with all their strength, all their wit so to do; but they were unable, because His hour had not yet come. And not always by the use of that particular phrase, but over and over again our Lord was looking forward toward some consummating, culminating hour which no man could hurry, and which no man could postpone, but which He did perpetually postpone until in the economy of God its set time should have come.

"We must work the works of Him that sent Me while it is day. The night cometh when no man can work" (John 9:4), was one of the profoundest sayings of Jesus in illuminating His own immediate ministry. It had larger values, I will readily admit, but often we miss the profoundest value because we fail to observe the first intention. There was an immediate application of that word, which the Revised Version helps us to appreciate by a change of number in the personal pronoun. "We"—He was speaking of Himself and His disciples—"We must work the works of Him that sent

Me while it is day; the night cometh," a time of darkness and desolation, "when no man can work," when you must stand aside from cooperation and fellowship with Me. That was the consummating hour to which He looked, the night of darkness that at last would come, in which no man could work, but God alone must work.

Now, in light of that all too rapid examination of a very definite movement manifest in the ministry of our Lord, we come to Gethsemane. The soldiers where about to lay hands on Him and lead Him away to Caiaphas and to Pilate and to Herod, and then to Pilate and to death. Before they did, He said, "This is your hour, and the power of darkness." The night, the hour postponed had arrived, and this was its character. From the sixth hour until the ninth hour there was darkness over all the land. We have no picture of the Son of God during those hours, no record of a word passing His lips. It was the period of the infinite silence, the period of the overwhelming darkness.

What, then, is this that Jesus said concerning the darkness? It was the hour of evil, it was the hour under the dominion of the powers of darkness. In those three hours we see the Savior in the midst of all that which resulted from the action of evil. Not without remarkable suggestiveness did the great apostle Paul speak in a letter written long afterwards of Satan as "prince of the power of the air" (Ephesians 2:2); and not without suggestiveness did he speak of him as presiding over the age as ruler of the darkness. Not without significance did John, the beloved apostle, when opening his gospel and writing concerning Jesus say that in Him was life, and the life was the light of men; that the light shineth in darkness, and the darkness apprehended it not, comprehended it not.

Neither the word *apprehended* nor the word *comprehended* means "understood" in this connection. The declaration is not that the darkness did not understand the light, but that the darkness did not extinguish the light. The apostle's declaration at the beginning of the gospel is that the light was always shining, and however deep and dense the darkness, it never succeeded in entirely extinguishing the light. The darkness apprehended it not—did not put it out. In that very negative declaration of the apostle you are brought face to face with the positive purpose of evil, with the purpose of Satan. What was Satan's supreme desire? To extinguish the Light. "There," said John of Jesus, "was the true Light . . . which lighteth every man, coming into the world" (John 1:9). Satan's purpose was to extinguish that Light.

From the very beginning of the shining of that Light, focused in history by the Incarnation, the one supreme purpose of the enemy was to apprehend it, to comprehend it, to extinguish it, to put it out. And in these three hours of darkness we are brought face to face with the time when all the force of evil was brought to bear on the soul of the Son of God, and all the unutterable intent and purpose of evil wrapped Him about in a darkness that is beyond our comprehension.

In that moment there was material darkness. It was the material symbol of the empire of sin. If the questioning of the heart shall become so material as to inquire—and I grant you it almost necessarily must—whether Satan did in some way actually produce the material darkness, I shall have to reply that I cannot tell, but I believe he did. I believe that by some action of those spiritual antagonisms, the world of principalities and powers, of which the early Christians were far more conscious than we are, and therefore more ready to fight with, under the captaincy and leadership of the prince of the power of the air, there was wrought out in material experience a symbol of the spiritual intention of hell.

I suggest for some quiet hour the study and examination of biblical symbolisms, and especially the use of the figure of darkness in biblical literature. For the purpose of illustration I confine myself entirely to the gospel of Matthew. Listen to these phrases, and immediately you will see how darkness is indeed a symbol of spiritual evil. "The people which sat in darkness" (4:16). "If thine eye be evil, thy whole body shall be full of darkness. If therefore the light that is in thee be darkness, how great is the darkness!" (6:23). "The sons of the kingdom shall be cast forth into the outer darkness" (8:12). "Cast ye out the unprofitable servant into the outer darkness" (25:30).

Wherever the word occurs in this gospel of Matthew, indeed wherever it occurs in the New Testament, or its equivalent in the Old, it is the symbol of spiritual evil in its issue and in its ultimate. Darkness is the twin sister of death. Death and darkness express the ultimate in evil. And in this hour, when the Lord Himself was passing to death, there was darkness. That material darkness which impressed the evangelists and the multitudes, and changed their attitude of mind toward Him, was but the outward and visible sign of the more mysterious and unfathomable spiritual darkness into the midst of which He had passed. Through the channel of His earthly life, all spiritual things were having material manifestation. The Incarnation itself was but the working out into human observation of the truth concerning God. And now, in the hour of the dying of the Son of God, in that infinite, awful mystery, spiritual evil had its material manifestation in the darkness that settled over all the land. The darkness was of Satan; it was coincident with the ultimate in the suffering of the Son of God.

The Passing of the Darkness

And now, before we ask the most difficult of all questions concerning the transaction of the darkness, in preparation for that inquiry, let us look once more at that at which we have already glanced, the passing of the darkness. In order that we may understand, let us listen again to the four words that passed the lips of the Lord beyond the ninth hour when the darkness was passing away and the light of material day was again breaking through on the green hill, on the cross, and on all those Judaean lands. Notice reverently, then, the four cries that escaped His lips, and divide them, as they most certainly are divided, into two groups, the first two and the second two.

The first cry was the expression of a backward thought. "My God, My God, why didst Thou forsake Me?" It was the call of Jesus as He emerged from the darkness, and from all that happened therein, of which no single word is actually written. It was in itself a revelation, like a flash of light piercing the darkness. "My God, My God, why didst Thou forsake Me?"

In the next word we have the expression of His immediate experience, of that of which in His humanity He became then supremely conscious, "I thirst."

Almost immediately following it we have another expression of His immediate experience, that of which in the essential mystery of His Being He was conscious, "It is finished."

The final word described a forward glance. As the first word beyond the darkness expressed the backward thought, "My God, My God, why didst Thou forsake Me?" the last word expressed a forward confidence, "Father, into Thy hands I commend My spirit."

We have listened to these words simply in order that we may try to be near Him as the darkness passed, and with all reverence, by listening to Him, appreciate something of the thinking of His own mind. A backward thought, "My God, My God, why didst Thou forsake Me?" An immediate experience within human limitations, "I thirst." Spiritual accomplishment, "It is finished." Then the future, the glorious future, "Father into Thy hands I commend My Spirit." Then He died, not of a broken heart, not of human brutality, not of murder by human hands; but of His own volition He yielded up the Ghost, and His Spirit, commended to God, passed to God. The death that saves was not that physical dissolution, but the infinite spiritual mystery of the three hours and the darkness, which being passed, He Himself did say, "It is finished."

In all that remained of the story beyond the hours of darkness, we have no record of any word uttered by the foes of Jesus. They were not present, or they seem not to have been, during that time. Indeed, it is something to be meditated with thankfulness of heart that no rude hand ever touched the body of the dead Christ. After the darkness, beyond the death and the dismissal of the spirit, they were loving disciple hands that took Him from the cross, wrapped Him round, and buried Him, giving Him the temporary resting place of a garden tomb. In death He was wonderfully preserved from all dishonor. The foes of Jesus seem to have withdrawn. Satan seems to have been absent.

Where was Satan? There is no answer in the records of the evangelists, and so I pass on to apostolic writings where I find this written concerning Christ: "Having put off from Himself the principalities and the powers, He made a show of them openly, triumphing over them in it" (Colossians 2:15). In the deep darkness, and in the midst of the silence, He triumphed over the forces of evil, the principalities and powers, and made a show of them openly by the cross, putting off from Himself all that assaulted Him in, and by, and through the darkness.

As the darkness passed, we again see the attitude of the people. They were arrested, they were touched with pity; there came illumination to them concerning the dying and the dead One, and a great fear possessed them.

The Transaction Within the Darkness

So, finally, we come to the most impossible subject of all, that of the transaction within the darkness. We admit that this can have no final exposition. We admit immediately that any even partial thing that may be said is incomplete. Every aspect of the infinite whole is larger than we can know. Every theory is of value, but all theories fail. This is not the place, nor would it be within the highest purpose of our worship, to attempt to prove that statement. But at least I may be permitted to say that, so far as I know, for 25 years I have been reading—with ever growing gratitude—great books on the Cross, and from each one I have gained something and every one I have at last laid down, saying as I did so, Yes, yes! All that, but more; something not reached, something not spoken!

God cannot finally be expressed in finite terms. "The stone which the builders rejected is become the head of the corner. This is the Lord's doing; it is marvelous in our eyes" (Matthew 21:42). It cannot be explained; it is the perpetual marvel. God must pity any man who thinks he understands this cross completely. God have mercy on any child of God if the day comes in which he has not to sing, "Love so amazing, so divine."

When the amazement dies out, it is not that the cross has been analyzed, but that the gazer upon it has become blind.

Yet we may gain some light from the words of the Lord as He emerged from the darkness, and the darkness itself was suggestive. We remember the word we have in Matthew 4:16: "The people which sat in darkness." Into that darkness the Son of God experimentally passed. "If thine eye be evil, thy whole body shall be full of darkness. If the light that is in thee be darkness, how great is that darkness!" (6:23). That darkness had passed into His heart, when He said, "My God, My God, why hast Thou forsaken Me?" (27:46). "The sons of the kingdom shall be cast forth into outer darkness" (8:12). The Son of God passed into that outer darkness.

That does not answer the inquiry as to what happened. I have no answer for that. Only this I know, that in that hour of darkness He passed into the place of the ultimate wrestling of evil in actual experience. There is light as I hear the final word, "Father, into Thy hands I commend My spirit" (Luke 23:46), for the word is a word which declares that whatever the transaction was, it was accomplished; that whatever the dying indicated, it was done.

Let us go a little further back, before the darkness, and listen to the chief priests who joined in the hellish clamor that beat on the suffering soul of the dying Savior. Among other things, they said, "He saved others; Himself He cannot save" (Matthew 27:42). That brings me nearer than anything else. Those were wonderful hours of the transmutation of basest things to high and noble things. That was the last taunt of His enemies; it has become the most illuminative word about the cross.

"He saved others; Himself He cannot." So they laughed at Him. Hear it again as a truth sublime and awful: because He saved others, He cannot save Himself. In order to save others He will not save Himself. Said the rabble, and said the rabbis joining in the unholy chorus, "Let Him come down from the cross" (27:42). He did not come down from the cross, He went up from the cross. The great Priest who already had burned the incense in the holiest place bore the symbolic mystery of His own shed blood into the holy place, but before He could do so, He passed into the darkness and abode in the silence three hours—a human measurement in order that we may somehow understand—and in those three hours He could not save Himself. That was because His heart was set upon saving others.

Why could He not save Himself? My question descends to the level of common, everyday human experience and capacity at its highest and its best. He might have saved Himself. He might never have gone to Gethsemane's garden. He might even in Gethsemane's garden have asked for twelve legions of angels, as He Himself did say. He might with one glance of His shining glory have swept the rabble from about the cross and descended to the deliverance of Himself. If He had spoken in terms of power He might have saved Himself. Why, then, was it that He could not save Himself? Because He is God, and because God is love, and love is never satisfied with the destruction of a sinner, but with the saving of a sinner. Love never finds its rest with holiness and righteousness vindicated by the annihilation of the things that oppose. Love will find its rest only when those who have been swept from righteousness and holiness are restored thereto and are remade in the image of the Father, God. That is why.

Yes, but once more. If that be true, then on the

ground of the mystery of the compulsion of the ineffable love of God in Christ, could love find no other way? Love could find no other way because sin knows no ending save by that way. The conscience of men demands that, the experience of men demands that. I base the twofold affirmation on the testimonies of the centuries and the millenniums. I base the affirmation on what I know within my own soul of sin.

Someone may say to me, "Cannot God forgive out of pure love?" I shall answer, "If He can, I cannot." If He could forgive me for the wrongs of which I am conscious, and that have left behind them their stain and pollution—if He could forgive me by simply saying, Never mind them, then I cannot so forgive myself. My conscience cries for a cleansing that is more than a sentiment of pity. Somehow, somewhere, in order that I may have forgiveness, there must be tragedy, something mightier than the devilish sin.

I do not know what happened in the darkness, but this I know, that as I have come to the cross and received the suggestions of its material unveiling, I have found my heart, my spirit, my life brought into a realm of healing spices, to the consciousness of the forgiveness of sins. And there is no other way and there is no other gospel of forgiveness.

In the darkness He saved not Himself, but He saved me. He declined to move toward His own deliverance in order that He might loose me from my sin. Out of the darkness has come a light. The word spoken to Cyrus long ago has been fulfilled in the spiritual glory to the Son of God, "I will give thee the treasures of darkness" (Isaiah 45:3). And because fulfilled to the Son of God by the Father who loved Him, and wrought with Him through the mystery of His forsaking, the word has been fulfilled also to the sons of God who are born not of blood, nor of man, nor of the will of the flesh, but of God. He gives us the treasures of darkness.

From the sixth hour until the ninth hour there was darkness over all the land, and from the darkness have come the treasures of pardon, and peace, of power, and of purity.

SCRIPTURE TEXT INDEX